The Invention of the Real

BY RICHARD STERN

Golk

Europe, or Up and Down with Baggish and Schreiber

In Any Case (reissued 1981 as The Chaleur Network)

Teeth, Dying and Other Matters

Stitch

Honey and Wax: The Powers and Pleasures of Narrative.

1968: A Short Novel, an Urban Idyll,
Five Stories and Two Trade Notes

The Books in Fred Hampton's Apartment

Other Men's Daughters

Natural Shocks

Packages

The Invention of the Real

The Invention of the Real

Richard Stern

The University of Georgia Press
Athens, Georgia

5/1982
Am. Lit.

Copyright © 1965, 1969, 1970, 1971, 1972, 1973,
1974, 1976, 1977, 1978, 1979, 1980, 1981, 1982
by Richard Stern

Published by the University of Georgia Press
Athens, Georgia 30602

Set in 11 on 14 Sabon
Designed by Sandra Strother

PRINTED IN THE UNITED STATES OF AMERICA

Library of Congress Cataloging in Publication Data

Stern, Richard G., 1928–
    The invention of the real.

    I. Title.
PS3569.T39A16   1982   818'.5403 81-10466
ISBN 0-8203-0589-8   AACR2

For Joan FitzGerald

When at the first I took my pen in hand
Thus for to write, I did not understand
That I at all should make a little book
In such a mode. Nay, I had undertook
To make another, which when almost done,
Before I was aware I this begun.
· ·
             . . . I only thought to make
I knew not what: nor did I undertake
Thereby to please my neighbor—no not I,
I did it mine own self to gratify.
· ·
For having now my method to the end,
Still as I pulled, it came; and so I penned
It down, until it came at last to be
For length and breadth the bigness which you see.
· ·
Some said, John, print it; others said, No.
Some said, It might do good; others said, No.
· ·
At last I thought, Since you are thus divided,
I print it will, and so the case decided.
· ·
    If thou wilt not read, let it alone;
Some love the meat, some love to pick the bone.
· ·
    May I not write in such a style as this?
In such a method too, and yet not miss
Mine end? . . . Why may it not be done?
· ·
Art thou forgetful? Wouldst thou remember
From New Year's Day to the last of December?
· ·
    Wouldst thou divert thyself from melancholy?
Wouldst thou be pleasant, yet be far from folly?
· ·
             . . . O then come hither,
And lay my book, thy head, and heart together.

JOHN BUNYAN,
"The Author's Apology for His Book"

Contents

Getting at Oneself   133

Acknowledgments

SOME OF THE CONTENTS OF THIS BOOK have appeared—usually in altered form—in the following publications: *American Scholar*; *Books Abroad*; *Book World* (*Chicago Tribune*); *Carleton Miscellany*; *Charlatan*; *Chicago*; *Chicago Daily News*; *Chicago Review*; *Chicago Sun-Times*; *College English*; *Encounter*; *The Georgia Review*; *Locations*; *National Review*; *New York Times*; *Paideuma*; *Quarry*; *Story Quarterly*; *Transatlantic Review*; *Tri-Quarterly*; *Yale Review*.

Preface

*T*HE INVENTION OF THE REAL follows soft upon an "orderly miscellany" called *The Books in Fred Hampton's Apartment*. A bouillabaisse of opinion, portraiture, gripe, theory, and self-revelation, little *Fred H.* did not reorder the wórld's appetite. Nonetheless, it worked up my palate—to which I now offer this successor. Here again essays jostle poems, reportage slides toward journal entries. "May not I write in such a style as this?" Why not, when dealing with this odd old subject of the real and its invention and expression, its makers and their limits, its public and its private faces?

Portraits

This section is a portrait gallery of sorts. Of very different sorts: an interview, a poem, comment on other portraits, a "sketch for a diptych," a profile. The profile is of an old pal. Naturally, there's much about him that isn't here. (He also owns a typewriter.) In some ways, the section is a bit like a reunion, and I feel like calling out to absentees, "Where are you Tom? Joan? Don? Phil? Why have I ne-glected you?" (You lucky dogs.)

A Memory or Two of Pound

THE YOUNGISH AMERICAN SCULPTRESS from Hemingway's suburb noticed him across the way in Cici's. "It must be someone." Not the first maker of stone heads who'd remarked that one. Cici's own headshape (and contents) is a Brancusi egg, but he agreed to find out the *professore*'s name. A menu was presented and signed "E. Pound." That afternoon, the sculptress told the American lecturer at Ca' Foscari. Much excitement: one did not expect to see the pillars of literature fleshed and ambulant.

I wrote Hugh Kenner, who supplied the pretext of a mission: ask him about the letters exchanged with Zukofsky; he'd once suggested they'd make a book and Zuk's interested. Fine, though I felt a slight Protocols-of-Zion discomfort in the particular mission.

One November day I walked the quiet *calli* back of the *Salute* knocking on doors, asking if a somewhat elderly American calling himself Pound lived there. I was pointed to Calle Querini, knocked and drew Olga Rudge's head from a third-floor window. "Who wants him?" "An admirer." The door was opened, I was inspected and passed in as relatively harmless. My five-year-old son, Andrew, followed.

Pound was flat on the bed, a blanket to his chin. The face was thinner, the beard sparser than my expectation, the face lined like no one else's, not the terrible morbid furrows of Auden, not the haphazard crevices of so many benign elders. For me, at least, these lines had the signatory look of individual engagements. Brow and cheeks, arcs and cross-hatches, with spars of eyebrow and beard hair curling out from what the sculptors worked with, the grand ovoid, the looping nasal triangle. Silent handshakes, Andrew at the head of the bed, I facing him. Over the silence—Olga Rudge, the one who misses it most, said it was richer than most talk—we made talk. We were both reading Aldo Palazzeschi, and I lent her one of his novels. She said Pound was reading the *Paradiso* aloud to her and also a book on microorganisms. "Beyond me." She brought tea and asked Pound if Andrew could have one of the initialed candied fruits he'd gotten for his birthday. The assent was slow and reluctant. (A great sweet-lover, he blushed when Miss Rudge joshed him about the gluttony segment of a French film they'd enjoyed.)

She was clearly the sea in which he existed. She cleaned, she shopped, she stoked the old stove (her thumb was split), she did the domestic medication. I would not, though, add a *D* to her name. There was always the strong charm, energy, wit, and ease of a person of accomplishment. "Domestic detail bores you, doesn't it, Ezra?" "No. You take care of it, Olga." In his mouth, the "Ol" of "Olga" was very full and protracted. "I shouldn't have let Olga go," he said when she'd left him with Joan FitzGerald (the sculptress) and me to go on an errand. There was the small panic of abandonment and worry in the full syllable.

Not that he wasn't a bit overwhelmed by the extraordinary care. "Eat your fish." "No." "It's not good?" "It's not good."

There was much joshing on both sides. I remember her description of his excruciating attempts to play the bassoon. She'd been a brilliant violinist. "Not that you can be a soloist in Italy. What Italian would *accompany* anyone?"

"Are you working now?" I asked him.

"Five minutes a day."

Now and then, the old hand would scoot to the table, scrabble up pencil and paper and make a note.

It was the beginning of a bad winter. He was as low as I guess he'd ever been. His teeth were bad (they were fixed up later), the cold was the worst since 1888, and he'd not recovered from a prostate operation or adjusted to living with the physical inconvenience. Even so, he read lots— there were new American novels on his table—and his literary judgements were always extraordinary, oblique, and unexpected.

The next time I came, he was sitting up and we talked easily for a couple of hours, though I felt like an extractor. He asked me what was going on. I told him what I knew. We disagreed about Eliot's plays—he liked them a lot—he spoke of the coherence in Eliot and Frost ("he wanted to be New England"), men who had their feet planted in one place, a fortunate and enviable thing. Nothing overwhelming, but every sentence clear, complete, and underwritten by thought. Remembering my expectations of what he would be, I thought, "This is exceptional sanity." Now and then, an odd remark fell out of silence: "Don't think pianos waited for the railroad." (Which may have had to do with cultural independence.)

Mostly, one sensed his instinct for occasion. It was not the reverse of simplicity. I think the word is probably *courtesy*: he acted fittingly. Which did not exclude play with social formula. "How are you today?" "Senile." Or to a visitor who said that X and Y asked to be remembered: "They're in no danger of being forgotten."

Memory, though, was the central worry of that year. My one emotional session with him turned on it. Joan had come back from America, and we went over for tea. There was some talk of Peggy Guggenheim, who lived down the way. I was going there for supper (the woman had fastened on my wife). I repeated something she'd told me about Pound in Paris days. Pound frowned, fretted a while, then said I was testing his memory, he was relieved to know for sure that what I said was fiction. The words froze the room. The two women talked a bit above them, then went downstairs. I told myself, "Well, he's shown his hand at last. I guess the stuff I've heard about him is so." I debated leaving him with a nod but went over to the bed, held out my hand, and said he was probably right, most social talk was a mix of persiflage and fiction, I was sorry to inflict it on him. He held my hand tight, then drew me down to the bed. My face was within a foot of his. The blue eyes were charged with— what? appeal? reaching out? "No," he said, in his almost-Scotch burred English. "Wrong. Wrong, wrong. I've always been wrong. Eighty-seven percent wrong. I never recognize benevolence."

It was something, but I managed to say that maybe he'd been wrong but that those who delighted to tell him he was weren't in the same league when it came to verity.

"You don't know what it's like," he said, "to get off on the wrong path. Not to remember."

I tried something comforting. "You've been on the bull's-eye plenty in your time."

"No," he said, "I've only left scattered notes. Haven't made anything clear."

I'd been reading him and mentioned things that were not only clear but radiant.

It was no time for mollification. He quoted something from Dante about imperfection, and there was more, some of which I didn't follow. The old man was touching bottom, holding on meanwhile to something human on the surface. After I don't know how much time, minutes perhaps, I withdrew—though I thought after I should have stayed with him till he came all the way back. I touched his hand for goodby.

I didn't see him much. Occasionally we'd meet by chance in the piazza—no welcoming smile was sweeter—or have ice cream on the Zattere with one of the children and Miss Rudge. When my wife came with me, he spruced up, throwing the blanket over his feet, sitting up straight in bed. He talked about his version of the *Women of Trachis* ("not much Sophocles there"), of walks in France and Venice. By the time I left in the spring of '63, Joan had made a wonderful bronze of his head (which I now own). He loved it, preferring it to the one she made later (which is in the National Portrait Gallery in Washington).

I'd occasionally send him a card—never answered but supposedly welcomed. A card Miss Rudge said he especially appreciated was a Rossellini Madonna and Child sent at Easter "as a bit of spiritual Esperanto from a skeptic Jew to a skeptic Confucian."

We never talked directly about Jews. His anti-Semitism had been—I think—a wicked rhetorical habit, part populist, part the casual snobbery of upper-middle-class Europe and America. During his worst days, it was reinforced by the slime fury dredged up by the Nazis. It was attached to his historically flawed notions of usury and, now and then, to that nineteenth-century orthodoxy which had a Hebraic cast. Miss Rudge spoke deliberately of his Jewish friends, and I noted the dedication of *Guide to Kulchur* (to Bunting and Zukofsky). I doubt that he had ever prejudged a human being or a work on racial grounds.

But who knows? He welcomed all sorts of things one didn't think he would. A prize that year from *Poetry* was enormously important to him. He told me he'd never received any prizes and that none of his recommendations for them was ever heeded. This was surely exaggerated, but he'd been in bureaucratic toils in a way I hadn't, and isolation and persecution were near and awful facts for him.

I remember all sorts of other things, none earth-shaking. I came back from Rimini full of amazed disgust for the colossal chutzpah of Sigismundo Malatesta, one of his heroes. "I was just trying to set down the other side of the story," he responded. "I don't think there's anything actually *wrong* in there." ("There" was the *Cantos*.) Later, though, reading from them, he'd occasionally say, "No, that isn't right."

When I saw him again in the fall of '65, he was much cheerier. More of the world had forgiven him, he was honored here and there. We took a marvelous gondola ride to his favorite places. (Offering the one cushioned seat to Miss Rudge, he heard her quote him: "'They will come no more,/The old men with beautiful manners.'") We exchanged stories about Hyde Park Corner speakers. (I'd just come from there with a handful.) He remembered an atheist about 1906 describing Hell, "the walls a mile thick and a mile 'igh, and wot hi wants to know is 'ow they get in." Miss Rudge wondered what presents they should carry to Paris. "I believe lace and handkerchiefs are still considered indispensable." He characterized a few locals: "X is a fool and a charlatan." He walked, drank Scotch, went to operas and concerts.

His last years were, I'm told, even pleasanter. He was in generally good spirits, as he was—Joan told me—the night he died. His last birthday party was first rate: cookies, candies, neighboring children, friends, the works. Shortly after it, he was in some discomfort and Miss Rudge got him to the hospital near San Zanipolo. She and Joan talked with him for hours. He was restless, saw no reason to be there. Joan went back to Calle Querini for his pajamas and to call his daughter, just in case. (Hospitals are hospitals.) He dozed off and died. One blue eye remained open. The coffin was shut on it. He was taken to San Giorgio and remained that night between four lit tapers. To the brief services—conducted by a priest from San Giorgio and another from San Vio—came not only friends and family but *contadini* from Rapallo. The coffin went in the black gondola to San Michele, where it lies close to Stravinsky's in one of the few uncrowded sections of the burial island. The stone—lettered by Joan FitzGerald—says only "Ezra Pound."

There are fewer poems in this book than I'd like. The gentle voice of the editor, himself a poet, mastered my—insecure—claims for them. "Print your lousy poems and they'll crush you," went the voice.

Poor poems.

Still, I wonder. Are they so lousy? O.K., they don't roar up from my soul's depth, but they do come from somewhere in me. And God knows I worked on them. Nor am I completely walled in by vanity: they've all been printed by sensitive editors. I'm not then their only fan.

Final argument: they belong in this book; they express notions which either come out differently in prose or aren't handled there at all.

Reader, if they bore, annoy or repel, pass over them quickly. (They're few. They're short.) But if you enjoy them, if you feel them softening, enlarging or otherwise transmuting the text, reader, take a piece of my heart.

Venetians

1.
The *pensione*'s full.
Signor Cici, head abob,
goes from table to table,
trying to guess if all goes well.
Once his hand flops in a bowl of soup;
He stammers pardon in Venetian,
and returns to his boiled chicken legs,
his golden, quotidian delight.

Things have gone so well,
he buys a motorboat.
But the driver's test!
"What do you do when nearing a boat in the fog?"
"'*Ente*." *
"*Niente? Niente?*"
"'*Ente. Non esco l'ebbia*."
He doesn't drive in the 'og.

His place is used by English
uppercrust dykes
as hideout from the *Danieli* circuit.
Signor Cici sits in his moored boat
pondering under his commodore's cap:
"It must be all right.
"After all, a *contessa*."

2.
Signora Lydia's daughter, five months gone,
has married in the *Redentore*.
With her puzzled groom
she cruises under the Bridge of Sighs
while the photographer snaps
her best seconds.

At the *trattoria*, Signora Lydia's
shoeless left foot
relaxes under white cloth.
Snapped, it becomes a souvenir.

* Cici omits initial consonants (see Journal entry for January 6, 1963, in this volume). *Niente* means "nothing." *Non esco l'ebbia* is translated in the following line.

Fortunato's son was married
in *San Giorgio degli Schiavoni.*
Roses and carnations
brushed the Carpaccios.
For six months, he described
the wedding menu.
"Did I mention the black olives?"

3.
Up the *fondamenta* from Cici's
the old American poet lies in bed.
He feels the winter terribly.
Nothing is clear anymore.
Body a mess, mind foggy.
Once in two weeks, a phrase zeros in,
three or four words that make sense.
He gets them down before the chill,
the Venetian chill, abducts their warmth.

Bellow's Moving Day

*A*N UNINSPIRED DAY, neither hot nor cold, bright nor murky, a gray, medium October day, the thunder god's day (but who regards old Norse fiction in Chicago?).

Two blue trucks pincer an ivory van long as a small tunnel in front of a dark-glassed, mushroom-soup-colored high-rise on Dorchester Avenue. On the sidewalk, padded tables, armchairs, sofas, chiffoniers. Fetching and hauling heavy loads does not leave much energy for joyous reflection, but Hallett's Gibralter-shouldered movers seem at least bemused by this morning's job. "The cameras was waiting when we got here," one tells me. Another, boy-cheeked, Genghis-mustached, says the phones have been ringing all morning.

On the thirteenth floor, I walk in the open door with the congratulatory bottle and find the departing proprietor, phone to ear, on a scalloped loveseat by the broad window. The view is terrific: the cheery American Gothic towers of the University of Chicago with all their courts and fields and grassy quadrangles, the coppery knuckles of the Loop down—north—to the right, the stony, El-bound lumps of Woodlawn beyond the green flanks of the Midway Plaisance, where, eighty-odd years ago, Henry Adams derived from the machine displays of the Columbian Exposition the notion that the dynamo was a rough equivalent of the Virgin Mary as far as motive power went.

Bellow is in a turtleneck the color of the Midway. He's tired; the face, which can alter more and more quickly than any I've seen, is now drawn, and, if not quartered, grooved, pallid, a bit puffy at eyes and throat. ("If I don't look well, I look busted," says Charles Citrine in *Hum-*

boldt's Gift.) The news birds have been flying around for days, conveying rumor, asking to *be there as you hear the news*. He read Stendhal to prepare for the afternoon class, his wife, Alexandra, went about her mathematics, this morning a Reuters man waked him with the actual announcement off the wires, he drove a dozen miles south to open the apartment for the movers, and now, between phone bouts, directs which pieces go into storage, which to her lakeside apartment. He's moving to save her the long drive to Northwestern, where she is professor of mathematics. A month ago, gloomy, briefly out of the stream of invention where he's spent most mornings of the last forty-odd years, he described that view as "beautiful void in front, filthy void behind." And, "Don't let me molder." Genuine—I could tell from the low set of the fedora—but for years I have seen this old friend convert depression, fury, whatever, into marvelous literary comedy. Which doesn't make the feelings easier to feel. Indeed, the problem is holding on to them, getting more of them, until they break open on the understanding and you can find words for at least their fragments.

"Why not?" he says to the unusual—unique?—morning bottle. "*Mumm's* the word," say I. He finds a couple of unpacked highball glasses, and we raise them to the dynamite king's bequest. "Alexandra says there's no prize in mathematics because Nobel's wife's lover was a mathematician." A drop of story juice even in this old rind.

The oldest of his three sons calls from San Francisco. "Thank you, Greg. Now you know why I was after you to be quiet thirty years ago. . . . You're a good son, I love you." He speaks to his daughter-in-law, inquires after his granddaughter, "a true Bellow," the great dark eyes, the straight nose.

Earlier, his sister had telephoned and, recalling their father's dismay at Saul's desire to be a writer, wept. Now he says dreamily, "That antique." Ten times a year, Moses Herzog's father recited his chronicle of failure. "Put out at four years old to study, away from home. Eaten by lice. Half-starved in the Yeshivah . . . worked in Kremenchug for his aunt . . . had a fool's paradise in Petersburg for ten years, on forged papers . . . sat in prison with common criminals. Escaped to America. Starved. Cleaned stables. Begged. Lived in fear. A *baal-chov*—always a debtor. . . . Taking in drunken boarders. His wife a servant." Brilliant, learned, half-loony Moses, trying to slip out from the weight of these memories, to make sense of them, thinks, "But all these are antiquities—yes, Jewish antiquities, originating in the Bible, in a Biblical sense of personal experience and destiny. What happened during the war abolished Father Herzog's claim to exceptional suffering. We are on a more brutal standard now, a new terminal standard, indifferent to persons. . . . Personalities are good only for comic relief. But I am still a slave to Papa's pain."

Tom Guinzberg, Bellow's American publisher, calls, is reminded the author has been with Viking since '48. "One publisher, two—no, three wives." Like Chicago, Viking is another loyalty, another target. ("*Humboldt* was bound so poorly it wouldn't stand up on a shelf.") And now, "They're used to this. They have the English-language Nobels. Patrick White. Steinbeck. Look what I found." From a delicate, brass-figured, many-drawered mahogany desk, he fetches a white pamphlet: Steinbeck's Nobel Prize lecture, 1962, inscribed to "Saul Bellow. You're next." "He was right. Poor fellow, It was a burden on him. He took it seriously, felt he didn't live up to it. Well, it must mean something. At least I don't have to worry any more about recognition. Not a total loss. *Spurlos versenkt*." (Sunk, without a trace.)

A few years ago, after some other international award, Bellow said, "All I started out to do was show up my brothers. I didn't have to go this far." The magic third son, the baby, pampered by his mother (whom he watched die when he was fifteen—"Her hands turned blue, she saw me notice them"), today overwhelming his brothers and sister with memories for which they have less use. Brother Morris, greatly loved, and grandly described, redescribed, and re-created in Bellow's books, calls later from Georgia—he too has just moved, to accommodate his wife's horses—he has big plans for Stockholm. A dozen years ago, after the inked galleys of *Herzog* were stolen in a post-office heist by thieves who drove off in a yellow Cadillac and were not difficult to locate, Bellow got a late call from someone who said he'd sell him back the galleys—they should meet at midnight under the El tracks. Then a horse laugh. "Morris" (who'd seen the newspapers). In his way, too, Morris has been "a slave to Papa's pain." Since boyhood, he has been a lordly manipulator, trader, money-maker and -loser; occasionally he invests some of his younger brother's money. As does his son, another wizard of currency.

Investments, deals, arrangements, the mean grandeur and farce of business have been no small part of Bellow's fiction. About it, he is almost as knowledgeable as Dreiser, but less awed, and both more amused and more disturbed.

Since *Herzog*, he himself has been well off, which he enjoys as a fact, just as he enjoys the new range it supplies. Generous, even prodigal, he is also careful, alert to genteel swindle, to the harsh equations of money and love. In his story "The Old System," a dying sister offers to make up with and see her brother if he gives her twenty thousand dollars. Desperate to see her, the religious, memory-drunk old finagler coughs up. "As soon as he handed over the money, he felt no more concern for it. It was nothing." The withered, belly-swollen, tube-tied sister sweeps the money away and tries to embrace him. All this is recalled by Dr. Braun, their young cousin, who wonders about the use of all this love-and-money passion, this "crude circus of feelings" which humans tell themselves makes them human. "Perhaps the cold eye was better." Yet he can't stop going over and over the old stories. Why? Is he a depressive? "Depressives cannot surrender childhood—not even the pains of childhood," thinks Herzog who tries to explain this same peculiar haunting of the past. What can you get from it? Understanding? Hardly. Maybe "an intimation of understanding," a small *maybe* that humankind might, just might "comprehend why it lived." And Dr. Braun goes out to look at the inhuman stars, those "things cast outward by a great begetting spasm billions of years ago."

Stars and sisters, thugs, thinkers, lawyers, rabbis, thieves, philosophers, morticians, doctors, equities, and passions. It isn't by dodging the world's racket that a Bellow lives or writes. By equaling it, yes: "The poet is what he is in himself, because a voice sounds in his soul which has a power equal to the power of societies." At least, this is what Charles Citrine learns from the poet Humboldt. "You don't make yourself interesting through madness, eccentricity or anything of the sort, but because you have the power to cancel the world's distraction, activity, noise, and become fit to hear the essence of things." One lives, things happen, one feels, understands, puts words on them. The odd process is analogous to the slow conversion of living matter into fuel. (Perhaps Bellow carries on his father's coal business in another mode.) In any case, Bellow does not hole up in a cave with a cat, hanging on to the world with a radio and the mail. His books are the world felt by a very special, continuously exercised, very fervent mentality. Unlike much contemporary fiction, his books are not worked out as scores for critical orchestras to turn into sound. Nor is he a fictional factory, a graphomaniacal rambler discharging narrative seizures in annual volumes.

His books are slow in coming because each contains a clearing of a mental and emotional forest. The clearance is done by a central character for whom Bellow has had ever-greater requirements. He is discontented with his early heroes who had "no real appetite for high life, only scorn of low life." "All my books are about education and have therefore a somewhat boyish spirit. Bring characters to the conclusions of their errors and leave them prepared to take the first step." So each book leaves him at the threshold of the next, which must go deeper, further, be less fuzzy-minded. No easy assignment.

Humboldt's Gift was eight or so years in the actual works. It began as most of the books do, *out there*, with an event, a feeling about an event. Bellow's old friend, the poet Delmore Schwartz, had died in squalor. Bellow had seen him on the street some weeks earlier and could not face him. He began a memoir—so Delmore would not be *spurlos versenkt?*—which, in a month, turned fictional, became a subject, a story: it was important who remembered and why, who survived, how, and why. But the central sensibility, the survivor, was unsatisfactory. The book was written over and over with different centers, once or twice without them. Meanwhile—luckily, I think—Humboldt and Humboldt's world grew. (He is the largest second banana in Bellow's fiction.) Yet Bellow did not want to make the "mistake" he'd made with *The Adventures of Augie March*. "Augie was excited by the memory of someone I knew in childhood, who disappeared and whom I never saw again. I thought I'd imagine what his life might have been like. What happened was that I drew on a lesson I learned from Sherwood Anderson and other American innocents and pseudo-innocents. Having adopted the role of the innocent, I couldn't doff it. So the book remained ingenuous. I couldn't introduce a shrewd contrast without surrendering the original given. Therefore, as I went on, I felt trapped in an affectation of innocence." Stymied by the Humboldt book, Bellow tried other things. One was a story begun after hearing that his old pal from Tuley High, Oscar Tarkov, had spotted a pickpocket working the Broadway trolleys and didn't know what to do about it. Something here linked up with the lives of some Polish Jews Bellow met in New York and Cracow, and Mr. Sammler, who looks like one of them, came into existence to control and express Bellow's feelings about such things as the violence-hunger and civil rot which were conspicuous facts of the late sixties. Or was it Sammler who needed such feelings, and such events, and was more likely to have them? Perhaps there was a confusion here which led to or resulted from rushing the book. Bellow is dissatisfied with *Mr. Sammler's Planet*, feels that "like *Augie*, it dealt with a new state of mind but wasn't under control. I should have gone all out with it." As disciplined as anyone I know, as conscious of the longer perspective, Bellow is subject like anyone else to extra-literary pressures, need for response, need to know if his "illusions" catch fire.

Bellow had also worked on another book, "an easy, funny book," based somewhat on the life and stories of his old pal, paddleball partner, and sometime traveling fellow, David Pelz, a Gary contractor, health freak, and bon vivant. They went off to Africa on some sort of industrial diamond hunt, and ended up—with Saul Steinberg—cruising toward Murchison Falls, Bellow euphorically—and rarely—high on hashish, enchanted with the beautiful crocodiles, green and white under the water. Pelz's character and misadventures melted into the book about Humboldt, and another, deeper Bellovian narrator came along to connect the two worlds. Charles Citrine—a sharpening of the name of Louis Sidrin, another old friend—shuttles between New York and Chicago, past and present, takes his instructions and his lumps from the poet Humboldt and such reality-professors as divorce attorneys, fragrant ladies, and fastidious thugs. Like the Bellow heroes since Augie, Charley is a Columbus of the Absolute (Augie was a "Columbus of those near-at-hand") whose ear is cocked for its supernal music, that is, for a cosmic guarantee of permanent significance, permanent enchantment. In *Humboldt's Gift* this music is largely supplied by the books of Rudolf Steiner, about whom Bellow had read in a book by the English critic Owen Barfield. (Most intelligent literary critics are unreceptive to such telegraphy; they regard Steiner as a cosmic four-flusher, but Bellow thinks he was an authentic visionary, and he attends Steiner Society meetings in Chicago today.)

The final push *Humboldt* needed came from the happiness Bellow found in meeting, courting and marrying Alexandra, the beautiful brown-eyed Rumanian mathematician. Not that Bellow had lived like Saint Anthony in the years since his last, endlessly protracted divorce. "What a woman-filled life I always led," says Citrine. Bellow is ravished by Alexandra's exotic, mathematic celebrity and trails her on the lecture and conference circuit—Berkeley, the two Cambridges, Austin, Jerusalem. Though once, marooned among topologists for a rainy week in the Black Forest, he did not think her world made for ideal society. "Since I've never understood women anyway, I finally married one who's really mysterious."

In a way, Bellow himself is not mysterious. Not now, anyway, after he has spelled out versions of himself on several thousand public pages. He is said to be exceptionally sensitive to criticism, but his books at least are full of what amounts to self-accusation, some of it put into the slanging mouths of enemies, friends, wives. Naturally he surmounts his created alter egos; perhaps he is simpler than any of them, because certain essential reactions and decisions were made very early. Like Bellow, Citrine spent some of "my eighth year in the public ward of a TB sanitarium. . . . I became very thoughtful there and I think that my disease of the lungs passed over into an emotional disorder so that I sometimes felt, and still feel, poisoned by eagerness, a congestion of tender impulses together with fever and enthusiastic dizziness."

The eagerness and the tenderness persist, the openness to sensation, to the new and uncatalogued. They are part of the delicate machinery inside a Bellow fortress which is manned by learning, skepticism, comparison, and an extraordinarily sensuous memory for experience and for literature. Bellow is not particularly proud of this gift, but he can be defensive about it. He cited Nietzsche one night; Hannah Arendt challenged the citation. Bellow went home, spent hours hunting it down, copied and mailed it to her the same night.

American literary history is full of writers who for one reason or another—isolation, philistinism, celebrity rapidly made and rapidly pulverized, and the pressure of constant invention—have thrown in the literary towel after five, ten, or fifteen years. There is, as well, an insecurity built into the lives of fiction writers and poets. It has to do with confusing the intensity and logic of their stories and poems with the inertness and drift of so much life. The writer often puts excessive pressure on his experience: breakfast tables become theaters, the casual encounter isn't so casual. It makes for trouble, but then trouble makes for books—or for drink, evasion, breakdown, suicide. How many American writers have published first-rate imaginative books over a thirty-year period? Perhaps three, Henry James, Faulkner, and now Bellow.

So here is the white-haired, compact, handsome prince of American literature strolling through Hyde Park, Chicago, in one of Armando's splendid suits, candy-striped shirt from the Burlington Arcade, Hermès tie, his velvety fedora jaunty with a Patagonian eaglet's feather in the braid. The slightly hooded eye is taking in the street, the tongue is ready to greet or to annihilate. (Part of the fortress? Part of the static between broadcasts?) A woman complains an old lover came on her like a steamroller. Bellow: "Did you have to lay down the asphalt?" A young waitress sullenly slaps down his hamburger at The Eagle: "Puberty and menopause hit her at the same time." A celebrated poet goes off to Caracas with a pride of critics: "They carry him around like a piece of the true cross." On eminent friends or former colleagues: "the Bettelheim of the Republic"; "Tillich the Toiler." On Bloomsbury: "that Himalaya of molehills." After trying to moderate a difficult meeting with his gifted, sensitive colleagues on the Committee on Social Thought: "All those prima donnas and not one song." Back from one of the fifty-odd lectures given over the globe these past years, he describes the small town: "In *Fontemara*, the priest explains what it's like to be a peasant: 'First, there's the king, then the nobility, then the gentry, then the merchants, the tradesmen, the laborers. Then there's nothing, and again nothing, and once more nothing. Then there's the peasants.' DeKalb's the third nothing."

Always new books, old books, high talk and intimate talk, not so much gossip as the marrow of lives. "The first time I met Saul," said Angus Wilson, the English novelist, "we walked all around Rome talking about ourselves. I told him everything about myself, things I'd never told my closest friends. When we got back to the hotel and said goodby, he said, 'That was nice, but next time, we'll really have to let our hair down.'"

Bellow's talk is full of opinion as well as wit and observation, but he has not published his opinions—his lectures—in book form. "I was influenced by Schopenhauer's 'Essay on Style.' 'You can debate opinion, not imagination.' Why publish opinion?" His new book, *To Jerusalem and Back*, is mostly a heap of other people's fascinating opinions beating themselves against the facts of the city, its people, and their own beings and behavior. There is also, though, straight opinion, and it may be that now Bellow feels he should speak out about certain things without submitting them to the canons of imagination. "Tolstoy," he says, "was forced by art to be fair to Karenin. Then he threw art out." It's not likely that Bellow will become a Tolstoyan reformer or even a persistent advocate. Still, he has led a civic life, a social life, a reasonably public one as well as the life which counts most for him and what makes him count most. He thinks of doing a Jerusalem-type book on Chicago (another beleaguered treasury?).

Does he now feel the need to declare himself directly? And does that mean that the maker of Herzog, Henderson, Humboldt (all those *h*'s, "as if I'm getting my breath") has completed his education? I doubt it.

In any case, on this moving day, as he directs the beautiful desk to the North Side, he says, "Maybe now, I can write something really good for a change."

May 1981. Bellow is finishing up his novel, The Dean's December. *"I'll have to take the ms. to Europe." (He's off to lecture at Oxford, has only one of his two lectures written.) "The last third's very rough. I've never written a book so fast." After Oxford, he has a week in Spain, then he'll try and see Beckett in Paris and our old pal Paolo Milano in Rome. "While Alexandra's with her mathematicians in the Black Forest, I'll work on it. And I'll do a lot on the galleys." "Is it funny?" "No. It's gloomy. Why not? It comes out of Chicago's gloom. The University won't like it either. But why should they?"*

A little snow has fallen in Bellow-land. Brother Morris's finagling got confused with fraternity, money was lost and there's chill between the brothers. Brother Sam, "sweet as always," also had business and then legal trouble. "You took all the brass rings." "The merry-go-round went too fast for them."

Still, Gregory's wife is expecting a second child, Juliet, the first, "is wonderful," the other boys are coming along, and he's ok. Though "I wish I could move back to Hyde Park. Do you realize that in six years, you haven't seen my apartment." (It's only four-and-a-half.)

We're hardly ever in Chicago at the same time."

"There's nothing up there but Alexandra and the lake. I can't even take a walk. Not that I'm up to many walks."

"You look fine." In a spring-colored, well-vented suit and a tie crowded with flowers.

"I twirl on my chinning bar. And do thirty or forty push-ups." No more handball.

The tongue is still one of the West's fastest. "She put the dish in 'fiendish.'" Of a certain critic: "The rat in Ararat." Of Z. "She's got too much spark. Better the park without the s." The new game on Block Bellow.

"Bellow in Five Hundred Words or Less"

FIVE HUNDRED WORDS FOR WHAT? Forty years' work, fifty thousand—odd hours of listening, thinking, forming, writing a dozen books which will not get washed away with the years' Diors or the decades' crises. There is no ordinary life, every mentality is unique, but the center of Bellow's novels is an extraordinary man. The man is not so much en route as arriving in a place whose maps don't correspond with what he sees and what he thinks. The Bellow man is usually told he's a dreamer, out of whack, and he gets in trouble all the time. There's always lots of trouble to get into. The place is full of poetic sharpies, intellectual wisenheimers, thugs posing as realists (the place is often Chicago, a Chicago transfigured by the Bellow Sound and Light Show). It's full of terrific women, large-eyed, heavy-legged, exceptionally fragrant. The hero is an emotional sucker. He requires enchantment and doesn't know that he supplies most of it himself. He's usually taken for a ride, but at the end he is as he was, by himself and full of resonant stillness. (The one Bellow heroine, Hattie—in the story "Leaving the Yellow House"—ends up willing the house to herself. There is no one else to trust.)

Balzac's heroes fight their way in and out of intrigues. Dostoevsky's tangle with ideological madmen. The Bellow hero fights windmills which look not like giants but like philosophers and wives. Still, it's beautiful country. Though the landscape seems filthy, gloomy, stony, the Bellow hero is as susceptible to the glory of industrial smog as an English poet to a Venetian sunset. In fact, the world's beauty outlasts everything else, con men, old pals, old streets, beautiful women, radiant ideas. It outlasts everything but the hero's memory, which becomes an inner cosmos, a cosmos with a divine flipside. Comedian to the depths, Bellow is a visionary who feels through the farcical spin of things the Unmoved Mover.

Borges on Borges

Reality favors symmetries and slight anachronisms.

JORGE LUIS BORGES, "The South"

This 1966 interview with Jorge Luis Borges became a calling card during a South American trip in March 1979. (It had been distributed by my sponsors.) Borges is the closest thing to a hero on the immense continent, respected to the point of worship even by those who don't read him or who detest his politics. (He defined democracy as "forty million imbeciles who elect another who strips them bare." The definition had some authority coming from a man who'd resigned his job the day after the elected Juan Peron took power.) In March 1979, eighty years old, he looked but did not feel well. ("I cannot hold out much longer," he told a Montevideo newspaper.) But we talked nonstop for two hours, literature, history, politics, jokes. Two days later, back from lectures in Rosario and Cordoba, I returned to the little apartment on Maipú to read Browning and Rossetti to him. He directed my friend Alane Rollings and me to the shelves where he'd placed the books a quarter of a century ago when his eyes functioned. (When I mentioned a poem of Jonson's, he said, "I have it, but don't know where.") The reading excited us immensely. He called out lines, said, "You see, you see, it's the Devil," or gripped my arm and cried, "Qué lindo, Qué lindo." The poem that rocked us was "Childe Roland to the Dark Tower Came." "Though I've never understood it."

As when a sick man very near to death

Seems dead indeed, and feels begin and end
The tears and takes the farewell of each friend . . .

Sitting next to the blind old fellow in the bare sitting
room, Roland's quest did not seem so mysterious, only
exciting beyond other expression.

When an old lady walked into the room, I did not,
would not stop. We were within that poem and couldn't
break out. Together Borges and I chanted the last line:
"Childe Roland to the Dark Tower came."

Then silence and drift back to the small room, the
yellow sofa, the white bookshelves. "There's some one
here," I said. The white-haired lady came to the risen
Borges. "Georgy," she said. "It's Esther." "Mi prima," he
told us. "Just back from Europe." It was time to go. "You
have given me a wonderful morning."

A year later, delicate and strong as ever, he was back in
the States, lecturing, or rather participating in endless
question-and-answer sessions, tossing his large-toothed,
blind smile toward the most intimate interrogators, an-
swering everything as if all would be known anyway. At
a party he recited German and Anglo-Saxon, asked what
people had read, what they thought. The Chicago host,
René da Costa, helped him to the bathroom, where, said
René, he recited, with the same scholarly exuberance, the
contents of toilet walls remembered from Paris, Rome, the
old days in Buenos Aires.

THE FOOLISH CEMENT PAVILION on Chicago's Midway is
the Center for Continuing Education. (What most continually educates is the industrial conference.) Off the low-

browed, submarine-dim corridors of the bottom level is the University of Chicago's Radio and Television Office. Here came Borges, slender, frail, his walk a bit askew, arm on that of a guide. His face is thin and long, the length emphasized by vertical grooves in the cheek flesh. A physically unforceful person, but with a gift for gesture and pose. Shaking hands, he draws close, his popped, muddled, gray-blue eyes inches from the shaker's face. "I make out lights and shadows." A gentle man who quickly touches the heart.

As Proust says of kings that they are *always* remarkable for simplicity, so fine writers who have been long praised are *always* egalitarian with younger colleagues. And when they are physically fragile, they develop Chaplinesque ways of charming the sting from that belligerence all noted men encounter. (Those who've seen the tiny Sartre scurrying about to offer and light cigarettes, pay for drinks, and sit smilingly alert while gallons of stupidity and vituperation inundate him will have seen a master example.)

The night before, Borges talked to a delighted audience about Whitman. A kindly speech, apparently recollected instead of read or improvised, somewhat soft and overextended, effulgent of Hispanic charm. The best of it was his memory of reading Whitman as a student in Geneva, "taking him like a cure." That remembered Whitman, the personality of *Leaves of Grass*, was "divine," a permanent presence like Quixote and Hamlet, a totally different being from the seedy Brooklyn newspaperman shuttling to Manhattan on the ferry.

Borges and I sit facing each other at a table in the little recording studio, microphone dangled above our noses. I apologize for my ignorance of Spanish, South America, the literature and customs of Hispanic culture. He replies that he will outdo me in ignorance. The control man signals, and here is much of what was recorded.

STERN: Last night you were talking of a multiplicity of Whitmans. Looking through your poems and stories, one sees at least a number of Borgeses. Sometimes, as in the charming *Borges and I*, you have written about this.

BORGES: I suppose we all are in a sense Dr. Jekylls and Mr. Hydes, any amount of Jekylls and any amount of Hydes, and a lot of others thrown in between.

STERN: For some years now, you have become a man-to-be-interviewed, a man who comments on Borges, or what Borges has done. Have you discovered a new Borges, a Borges created out of responses to attention?

BORGES: I hope I have, because when I was a young man I expected no one to read my stuff. So of course I could be as baroque as I liked. I used to write in a very far-fetched and stilted style. But now I've got to think of my readers and so, of course, that makes for good literary manners. All sorts of writers act in a different way. They try to be obscure and they generally succeed. Well, I have done my best to be clear and understandable and I think—so it is said—I have succeeded. Now I'm going to begin writing as soon as I get back to Buenos Aires, my home town, a book of straightforward short stories rather after the manner of Kipling's *Plain Tales from the Hills*. Not the last stories he wrote, those are very complex, very involved, and very sad also. I shall try to tell in a very straightforward way, plain stories. So I will try to get away from mazes, mirrors, from daggers, from tigers, because all those things now have become a bit of a bore to me. I will try to write a book so good that nobody will think I've written it. That's my aim.

STERN: Will the hills these tales come from be as they were for Kipling, remembered ones? With remembered people?

BORGES: Yes, they will be. I intend to go back to my childhood, because I think a writer should avoid contemporary subjects. If I set out to describe a particular café in a particular quarter of Buenos Aires, then people will find that I'm making all sort of mistakes, while if I write about what happened in a northern or southern slum of Buenos Aires some sixty years ago, nobody will care or remember. And that leaves me a little literary elbow room. I can dream at my ease, I can imagine things. I don't have to go into details. I don't have to become a historian or a newspaperman. I can just dream away. If the facts are essentially true, I don't have to worry about the circumstances. So my intention is to publish a book of some ten or fifteen short stories—let's say stories seven or eight pages long. And all of them will be quite clear. I've written one already.

STERN: At some time in your life perhaps the notion came to you that these tales, stories and poems were not only worked-out reveries but something committed to paper by an act. Though you say you expected no one to read your stuff.

BORGES: There were both these facts. Of course what was important was the fact that they were reveries or they were daydreams. Of course the fight of putting them onto paper gave me some trouble and lots of fun also. I remember when I was writing a rather grim story . . . I felt quite happy, because a writer should feel happy when he writes.

STERN: When he writes well, or thinks so.

BORGES: I wonder if one can speak about writing well. But

at my age I know my possibilities. I know I can't write things that are far better or far worse than the things I've already written. So I let myself go. I mean, at my age— I'm sixty-eight—I suppose I've really found my own voice, my own stand.

STERN: Yet you talk of writing in another way.

BORGES: Yes. I mean I want to write simple things, but at the same time, of course, I'm a writer. I can't get away from myself; I wish I could. Of course I'm tied down to my past.

STERN: You don't like the notion of art as an expression of personality.

BORGES: I wrote a story once, a kind of parable about a man who began a very large picture, and therein was a kind of map, for example, hills, horses, streams, fishes, and woods and towers and men and all sorts of things. And then when the last moment came, when the day of his death came, he found that he had been making a picture of himself. That is the case with most writers. We are supposed to be writing about different things. But really what is left at the end is our memory. I mean, what the reader finds at the end is our face, our features, though we are quite unaware of it. So this means that we can't run away from ourselves. But we don't have to try to—a search goes on in ourselves all the time.

STERN: You remember the James story of the figure in the carpet. You have another version of this somewhere. In a footnote, I think. You talk about the divine mind which adds up every gesture a man makes in his life and discerns its form with the same ease that lets us see three lines as a triangle. From sixty-eight years, fifty of writing stories and poems, what do you see in the relation between the writer's figure in the carpet and this life figure?

BORGES: One can hardly speak about those things. Every time I write I try to forget myself and to concentrate on the subject. Then I also think of the reader. I try to make the thing clear for him. What I've found out is that really I've been writing the same stuff over and over again. For example, I wrote a poem to a Saxon poet. I was thinking of the author of *The Wanderer*. Then a year afterwards I wrote a sonnet on the same subject without knowing it. And, thinking of stories of mine, I thought of two stories as quite different. And then a critic found out that though the setting was different, though it happened in different countries, the story was essentially the same.

STERN: Is this what may be meant by a Borges created by a critic's awareness?

BORGES: I think that in my case what I really know are my own limitations. I mean, I know that there are certain things that I cannot attempt. For example, I thought I had evolved a new plot. I told it to one of my friends who said, "Yes, that would be a fine plot but after all it's the same plot you already used," and then he mentioned a few stories I had written.

STERN: Do you think that the impulse to say "this is the same" or "I must try something new" is something which a writer living before, say, the Renaissance would have thought about?

BORGES: No, I suppose he wouldn't have thought about that because in those days they had a limited number of subjects. I don't think any knowledge was expected from a writer. And perhaps it was also good, because if you write a story whose plot is known to a reader then that saves you a lot of trouble because the reader knows all about the plot and you can concentrate on the details. In the case of Browning, for example, once he had told the plot in the first book, then he could go on to follow all the interrelations. All the many painters, for example, who have painted the Crucifixion have done the same thing.

STERN: Longinus said that much "modern"—first-century —literature was the deformed outgrowth of a search for novelty.

BORGES: What do you think of that? Longinus. Of course, Homer is the primitive writer. But, for example, I have known people who knew the Red Indians in my country, and they had no historic consciousness whatever. I remember one of our generals spoke to an Indian chief, and he said to him, "How awful it must be for you, how sorrowful to think that once you were the lords of the pampas, and then the white men came and now you are being driven out." And the Indian chief looked at him in amazement and said, "No. Ever since I was a boy I've seen white men." Then I remember that my grandmother told me they had slaves at home, and the slaves were staying with the family that owned them, of course. And I asked her if the slaves had any consciousness, if the slaves knew that their fathers had come from Africa and had been sold in the marketplace. She told me they had no knowledge of it whatever. Historic memory went back to their childhood, they had no notion about their grandfathers and so on, so they never knew they had come from Africa.

STERN: You spoke of your limitations. What are they, as you see them?

BORGES: For example, I would never think of attempting a novel, because I know I would get sick and tired of it before I had written the first chapter. Then I know that I can't attempt descriptions, and I think that psychologi-

cal analysis is something I should avoid, because I can't
do it. But if I can imagine a person, I think I would try
to show what is going on in his mind through his acts.
That's what happens in the Norse sagas. You're never
told anything about what the character is thinking, but
you find it out by his sayings or, still better, by his acts.

STERN: You've not felt an impulse to keep going, to keep on
with characters, to show them in relationship to other
characters?

BORGES: I had no special interest in that kind of novel. And
my friends tell me that there's something very childish
about me because I'm very interested in plots and an
intelligent man is supposed to have no use for plots. Of
course, once you really enjoy novels where very little
happens, where the characters are being idolized all the
time, that's the kind of book I would hardly read.

STERN: Stravinsky was asked last year [1967] what new
thing had come into literature in recent years. He said he
never would have guessed that people could make so
much of so little. He was praising Beckett and—

BORGES: But was it real praise?

STERN: My version sounds ironic, but his wasn't.

BORGES: I had a different experience, but still it's very en-
chanting. Let me tell it to you. I remember reading the
History of Argentine Literature by Ricardo Rojas. When
I looked over that book, eight volumes and perhaps utter
nothingness behind the volumes, I thought how intelligent this man must be in order to have written this
book and gotten away with it. He's written this book
and in spite of this, he's famous, he's respected.

STERN: The elephant mustn't let the ant write his epitaph.
Shall we talk about brevity as a determinant of other
artistic elements? We seldom talk of the consequences of

such things as brevity. Your tales and poems, as I know them, are brief.

BORGES: This is caused, of course, by laziness.

STERN: That may be its source, though I doubt it, since forty or fifty volumes testify at least to some form of energy.

BORGES: When I say laziness, I mean the task of taking a pen and writing. Of course, I don't think I'm lazy at thinking or dreaming. Writing's the kind of activity between thinking and dreaming. You have a dream at the outset and then somehow you have to pin it down.

STERN: Is there perhaps a kind of symmetry or absolutism that comes with brevity? I've noticed, looking through your pages, this kind of thing. You say, "Everybody made such and such a choice," or "No one dissented."

BORGES: Well, if I understand you, you mean that brevity makes for fairness.

STERN: No, I think not. Brevity makes for a kind of—

BORGES: Sweeping statements.

STERN: Yes.

BORGES: Yes, because if you're writing in a brief way and you interlard that with "so I think," or "perhaps," or "maybe," or "it is not impossible," it waters down and weakens what you're saying. So all that kind of thing is left to the reader. You simply give him a possible explanation of things or a statement that seems just possible to you and the reader of course has to turn it over in his mind.

STERN: One of the beauties of your stories and poems seems to be a clash between this—let's say—absoluteness and the enigmatic essence.

BORGES: I'll allow myself a confession. The confession is this: whenever I write a story I know that I have to work in some details, because people expect to be told, for example, what kind of flowers will be found, for example, in that particular kind of ground. Those details are required not by the naturalists but by the realists. Now when I've written a story, I generally ask my mother, "Now this happens in a tenement house. What kind of flowers would we have?" Or, "This happens in a *quinta* near Buenos Aires fifty years ago, what kind of flowers did they have?" And then my mother gives me full realistic details and I work them in. And then I go to somebody else, because I'm very absentminded and hardly notice such things. So when I write my stories there are practically no details and everything happens in the abstract. Well, if I know the reader may feel put out or perhaps he feels that he's floating about, then I give him a few details, but those are supplied by my family.

STERN: Well, one feels confidence in barely furnished stores; one isn't being swindled by decor. But then your stories are full of this odd tension or whatever it is, between the peculiar surety and the irreducible strangeness. Perhaps that is the Borges one wants to disinter from the various Borgeses.

BORGES: Well, you see, I'm not really a thinker. I'm a literary man and I have done my best to use the literary possibilities of philosophy. I'm not a philosopher myself, except in the sense of being very much puzzled with the world and with my own life. When people ask me, for example, if I really believe that the cosmic process will go on and will repeat itself, I feel that I have nothing at all to do with that. I have tried to apply the aesthetic possibilities, let's say, of the transmutation of souls or the fourth dimension, to literature to see what could be evolved from them. But really I would not think of myself as a thinker or philosopher, and I follow no particular school.

STERN: Yet certain philosophic filings are drawn to your magnet and not others.

BORGES: Well, that merely means I have my limits. I can be interested in certain subjects and not in others. For example, I've spent most of my life puzzling over time, the problem of time and of course my own identity. At least, they go together, because I feel that time is the stuff that I'm made of. But really, I have no particular theory about time. I have only felt it.

STERN: I read that one of your favorite Borges stories is "The South."

BORGES: I think it's the best story because, in any case, it's the most complex. It can be read in two ways. You may read it in a straightforward way and you may think that those things happen to a hero. Then, you may think there's a kind of moral behind it—the idea that he loved the south and in the end the south destroyed him. But there's another possibility, the possibility of the second half of the story which is hallucination. When the man is killed, he's not really killed. He died in the hospital, and though that was a dream, a kind of wishful thinking, that was the kind of death he would have liked to have—in the pampas with a knife in his hand being stabbed to death. That was what he was looking forward to all the time. So I've written that story in order that it would be read both ways. Of course, I was thinking of Henry James.

STERN: I know a bit of your relationship to Argentinian ancestors who figured with San Martin and others, and, that in your home there were swords on the walls.

BORGES: I've always felt a kind of wistfulness for epic. I

think, for example, that my grandfather was killed in a battle, that my great-grandfather fought the Spaniards, that another of my great-grandfathers fought the Brazilians, another fought the Red Indians. I think they had a fine destiny, but at the same time, perhaps they were not as aware of their destiny as I am, because they just went through it. But I am more aware of the epic significance of those destinies than they were, because they wanted to do their job and one of their jobs was to fight and be killed. That was all in a day's work.

STERN: So many of us praise what we feel we aren't.

BORGES: Even if we think of the things we lack—I mean if you're a healthy man you don't think about health. If a woman loves you, you think of something else. You're happy, but you don't have to worry about it. At the same time, when you write about any particular unhappiness that has come to you, you're in a sense liberating yourself. Even if it is a confession. For example, if I tell you something in confidence, at the moment I'm telling you the things, I am not there as the actual person, because in the very act of telling it, I'm somebody else. I'm somebody who can look at things from a distance, who can put it into words, who can tell it to somebody else.

STERN: But here, in "The South" there's this praise of a kind of honor which—

BORGES: Some sixty years ago in my country it was very important for a man to be brave or to be considered brave. I mean for a man to be a coward was a shame. I have known that feeling even, for example, among hoodlums, among very poor people. They were very ignorant, very limited men, and yet they all felt that to be a coward was the one unforgivable sin, the sin against the Holy Ghost. I have known, for example, the case of men defy-

ing a man they had never seen before simply because
they were sure that he was a brave man that was very
handy with his knife. They wanted to find out who was a
better man, so they would seek him out and sometimes
get killed for their pains simply because of—what? "I'm
as good a man as he is. If he's better than I am then let
him prove it." Nowadays, of course, all that has completely vanished in my country. Nobody cares about being brave. People care about being rich or about being
notorious, what people are talking about, and that sort
of thing.

I have thought of writing a story about a man who is
defied, who refuses a challenge, but he can do that because he knows he's not afraid. I thought of writing a
story about a man who is just a common hoodlum, and
then suddenly he sees through the utter vanity of being
brave, trying to live up to a reputation. Then he's a coward, people mock at him. Well, if he knows in his heart
that he's not afraid, he can take it. Of course, that's a
very difficult story to write because the whole thing has
to happen in his mind, unless, of course, there were two
stories, unless you were told the facts at first and then in
the end you might find out that the coward was really a
brave man, because he knew that he wasn't afraid.

STERN: I suppose the writers who count for us most offer
us the pleasures of realistic choices.

BORGES: I always get rather angry at those who speak
of reality on one side and of literature on the other as
though literature were not a part of reality. If you read a
book, it's as much of an experience as if you had trav-
eled, or if you were jilted. As for my stories, I have tried
to be loyal to them. I never write anything until I can

fully imagine it as possible. I'm not out for novelty or for astounding people. When I write something, it's because I know that I can really think about it. For example, if any of my characters say anything, then it's because I feel that those are the words they might have said. I try not to work in any other matter. I've been an enemy of the Communists, of the Nazis, of our dictator, when we had him, but I never let those opinions interfere with my work. When I'm writing a story or a poem, I'm not thinking of my opinions but of the possible implications of what I write. I try to be loyal, try to draw the thing as I see it, that's all. I don't think of a writer's opinions as really very valuable. For example, in the case of Kipling. I greatly admire Kipling. I don't think we have to worry about his political opinions.

STERN: The stories frequently contradict his directly expressed opinions.

BORGES: Yes, in the case of Kipling it's really remarkable. For example, in *Kim*, the finest characters are natives and he was quite unaware of that, because he was all the time speaking of the white man's burden and so on and yet the English characters are not very good.

STERN: They tear themselves apart in those hills where they don't belong.

BORGES: I wonder if Kipling knew that? He must have felt it. I wonder if we see him as he was. I think of Kipling as a really great writer.

STERN: Joyce said that the three great talents of the nineteenth century were Tolstoy, Kipling and—can you guess?

BORGES: No.

STERN: D'Annunzio.

BORGES: That's a comedown.

STERN: I haven't read enough to say.

BORGES: I've read very little D'Annunzio, and the very fact that I've read very little of him is my judgment of him. Tolstoy, Kipling and D'Annunzio. I wonder how you can admire all three. He had a very catholic mind.

STERN: Well, they all had immense energy, all were mad for straight stories. Once again, it's praising what one isn't.

BORGES: Well, I admire Tolstoy, of course, but D'Annunzio, I find him so bombastic. I think if a man has moral defects, they always find their way into his work. So I think if we write in purple patches all the time, I think it's a sin of vanity and that sin should hardly be forgiven. I think a writer should be able to write in a plain way, because if he's trying to impress a reader all the time, the reader, of course, finds it out and then he refuses to be impressed.

STERN: Do you think there is any good writing that comes from personal defect? Rage? Meanness?

BORGES: I wonder. Rage, of course. Now in the case of Oscar Wilde, for example—after all, he was writing purple patches all the time—but, at the same time, you feel that this was fun. That he wasn't taking them too seriously. There was also an Oscar Wilde who wrote *The Portrait of Dorian Grey*.

STERN: I suppose a life like Wilde's, in which one must always disguise and then always make something of one's disguises—

BORGES: Yes, but through the disguises, I think, a very level character.

STERN: And brave. You feel a man who disguises himself all the time must be a coward, but in Wilde's case you feel,

"Ah, there's real bravery."

BORGES: You remember what Chesterton wrote about Oscar Wilde. He had to sum him up in a page in one of the University Library books. Then he wrote a very fine book on *The Victorian Age in Literature*. And the book is full of epigrams, but they all make good points, and when he comes to Oscar Wilde he sums him up with these words, "Wilde was an Irish fighter." A thing that nobody ever thought of saying about Wilde. He says that he showed that in his trial and that all during his life he had been fighting really, fighting public opinion and at the same time getting hold of it. But the case of D'Annunzio I think is different because the purple patches one feels have been written without a smile, where in the case of Wilde you feel that he was smiling all the time or maybe laughing at what he was doing. It was a kind of joke.

STERN: You think D'Annunzio was emotionally simple or emotionally corrupt?

BORGES: I suppose both, but emotionally simple, I should say. I think Italians are clearer, but I don't think they're very subtle. I don't speak of all of them, but in my time I have found Italians practical men, all very cocksure of themselves and, of course, theatrical.

STERN: After this last World War, there's been a great deal of marvelously direct Italian art in movies and books. Mussolini may have used up an extra decade's quota of bombast.

BORGES: Well, I will make a last confession. I don't like Italian films. Whereas *Psycho* was a very fine film. I had a discussion with an Argentine critic. He told me the whole thing was a parody, that the whole thing was meant as a joke. I said, "Well, all love is a joke." But it's not being taken as a joke. It's a nightmare really. I suppose that comes from Jekyll and Hyde because they're the same essentially.

The tape ran out here. We continued talking at the table for half an hour or so. "It's not something for the machine," said Borges, "but conversation, une tranche de vie." We drank coffee from paper cups and he spoke of the screenplay he was writing with Bioy Casares and someone else. Invasion, *about six lazy men who succeed in repelling one. He'd written a couple of others over the years but nothing had come of them.*

We put on overcoats and went out. A gray day, halfway to snow. He wanted to walk back to the Quadrangle Club, where his wife was waiting. He talked of the difficulties of life in Argentina, the tiny salary he made as director of the National Library and professor of English and American literature ("You have to do it all in a semester"). "Less than a streetcleaner." Argentinians didn't think of themselves as South Americans. "Brazil is South America. You know, exotic, Indian, Negro."

"And Argentina?"

A laugh, the long, soft head scooping up towards mine. "A sort of Paris. Yes, where everything is derived, the Teatro Colon from the Opéra, the skyscrapers from, from Chicago. Everything imitation." He'd had troubles there under Peron. His mother was put under house arrest, his sister in prison, "a jail for prostitutes to increase the humiliation. It was a way of getting at me. She wrote that she was fine. That made me worry." He had the boyish directness that is the New World charm, gentler and more melancholy in its southern version. On the other hand, there was the strength of bravery and good heart in it.

At the club he did not want to be helped up the stairs.
He'd found ways of getting his bearings, and said goodby
with that intimate courtesy which makes some farewells
oddly sweet and painful.

*I met Mailer in 1958 here in Chicago and saw him
off and on for about a decade, the last time in his Brooklyn Heights house at a party he gave for the warriors
of the Columbia University sit-in. ("Boring heroes," was
his summary of them.) We've swum, played badminton,
sparred, smoked pot in an old orgone box, schmoosed,
argued in print and out, and lost track of each other. He
became more and more a celebrity, I more and more a
local burger, but an exchange here and there testifies to
old affection, if no longer intimacy. He concludes our
latest "fraternally yours" and this is how I feel as well.
One day I think I'll do a full-fledged portrait of him. I
don't know any that is not unhinged by belligerence, re-
sentment, or small-mindedness. (I don't exclude his peculiar self-portraits.) The willed and unwilled craziness, the
spunk, challenge, uncertainty, and small sadness in this
man beg for portraiture.*

Mailer

NORMAN MAILER is to American mental life what jet
planes are to transport: familiar, remarkable, ubiquitous,
powerful, rapid, noisy, and not altogether free of hot air.

Mailer's passport reads "novelist," and it's as a novelist
he began in 1948 with *The Naked and the Dead*, a marvelous book about the Pacific War that's full of Melvillean
rhetoric and specificity, organized by his version of Dos
Passos's version of *Ulysses*. If the form is creaky and the
men refurbished types, the book still feels accurate, lively,
intelligent, comic, and built rather than piled.

Three years later Mailer hauled in a gloomy political allegory called *Barbary Shore* (whose initials summarize the contents), and four years after that, a fine, quiet, off-Hollywood novel called *The Deer Park* which exhibited a little fatigue with its own method, the setting up and then subversion of stereotypes (of character and situation).

This was Mailer's last good novel, the last of any fiction for a time. His literary stock was low, he fiddled in disconnected Connecticut making nutty wooden constructions in a machine shop, playing badminton, drinking, smoking, and giving up drinking and smoking.

With the founding of the *Village Voice* in 1956, he apparently decided there were other ways to skin the literary cat. He turned out pieces about everything, pieces which got longer, stranger, more apocalyptic, and then, as the magazines and television realized he was a man liable to say and do almost anything short of being permanently cast out, more influential.

In 1959 Mailer stitched the miscellaneous pieces (essays, stories, interviews) with splendid bits of self-analysis into a new kind of autobiography, *Advertisements for Myself.**

The "myself" was plural; that was the book's subject.

One self was a Henry Adams–Mailer, a self-deprecating and vaunting critic of civilization; another was commonsensical, a comic knifer of pomposities, a sort of court fool; a third was the Great Reporter who made familiar ground unfamiliar until everyone conceded it to him; and finally, there was the old Demon of the Absolute, a pumping ranter scooping theoretical drool from dried-out Nietzschean waterholes and serving it up in the most

---

* The older brother of *Fred Hampton*; an interview I did with Mailer in 1958 is part of the book.

debased prose since Faulkner's *Fable* and Cozzens's *By Love Possessed.*

When editors didn't send Mailer to the wars, he made his own. He ran for mayor of New York, once unofficially and wildly, once brilliantly and straight. He stabbed a wife, he knifed old writer friends, he spooked (and thrilled) American gentry (presidential wives, transient heroes), he sent out a monkey self whenever he was bored or angry, often on camera.

His last movie (there are, I think, three) ends with Rip Torn improvising on Mailer's skull with a hammer while Mailer tries to rip off the actor's ear.

What remains are the books, some of which are terrific. If Mailer's reportage-maps are more detailed than the terrain mapped, this is what the true lensmen-discoverers of literature do; the terrain will be settled by others.

So if the astronauts in his lunar book, *Of a Fire on the Moon*, were not as complicated as his description of them, they might become so after reading it. (Neil Armstrong seems to have realized Mailer's description in himself; Frank Borman discarded it as more lunatic than lunar.)

Occasionally Mailer's subjects turned back on him. Muhammad Ali said no, Mailer's version of his Liston fights was wrong; and I don't imagine Jacqueline Kennedy accepted his version of her, though rumor has it she enjoyed his version of her late husband. (That featured Mailer's Dental Theory of Heroism: Kennedy, hauling a shipmate to safety with his teeth, has a molar sublimation of his life's fury which led to his becoming the cool-to-death existential hero. We'd better take another look at Mailer's dental grip on Torn's ear.)

In the best of the reportage books, *The Armies of the*

Night (1968), Mailer came up with his first full character, the poet Robert Lowell. Instead of creating somersaulted stereotypes, Mailer kept looking at what was really there, and the result was a complete man; not a "finished" character, because a living man[†] can't be finished, but someone complicated, explainable, memorable, and noble. In addition, the book supplies wonderful confrontations (the best a triangular glare-out in a paddy wagon).

Able to see, subtlize and render such things, what keeps Mailer from what he still appears to want, a wonderful novel, a fully imagined work?

My guess is that Mailer is without real sensuous power, without a unique—how can this be said?—sense of the flow, arrangement, and rhythm of events, a kind of music of feeling which generates—but isn't—meaning; and perhaps Mailer doesn't have the deep, secret patience, the sometimes clumsy tolerance which makes great novelists seem irrelevant to theory or their own personality, beyond any predisposition but the hunger to get people and scenes into formal, literary arrangements.

I won't swear by any of this. Perhaps it's not right to talk about it. Mailer is a national resource, a rare commodity. Should he go dry, he ought to be subsidized, decorated, given a villa in the country.

As much as anyone, he is the Secretary of Defense against National Boredom, and even if he's an occasional bore himself, he's worth a good many of us.

May God (Mailer's—that is, Nietzsche's—poor struggling Uncreature) speed him well.

[†]Lowell died in 1977. He said he was at first uneasy about the Mailer portrait, but by 1975—the last time I saw him—he admired it.

Faulkner in Genoa

In the fall of 1962 I was Fulbright professor at the University of Venice (then called Istituto Universitario di Venezia because the University of Padua wanted no full-fledged university competing with it and the minister of education was a Paduan). A splendid life for me. We lived in a little palazzo called the Gioconda next to a Palladio church, the Zitelle, on the Guidecca, an island across from the main Venetian island. The place included a uniformed butler, a pleasant young red-haired fellow who did the cleaning, assembled the tubing (which failed to dent the chill in this coldest of Venetian winters) and spent much of the day with a telescope watching his boy friend, a cameriere in a palazzo across the canal. My wife cooked lunch for Ennio except when he wished to show us how to prepare one of his special pasta dishes. After all, he was a cameriere, not a cook. He did "serve us" in the little bemuralled slot of dining room.

"Us" was my middle son, Andy, home from kindergarten in his white smock (grembiule), my wife, and I. The baby, Nick, was fed by signora Lydia, who wheeled him up and down the fondamenta and took him with her when she played tombola with our neighbor, signora Olga. The two older children (Kate, eleven, and Chris, twelve) were in the Salesian Sisters' School. Every morning they went across the canal in their black smocks and returned at four. Kate was quite happy, got religion, and loved her Sister, suora Emmanuele. (Ten years later, she walked into Sister Emmanuele's class, which rose in unison to call, "Ahh, Kati.") Chris dropped out after Sister Emmanuele explained that Lincoln was axed to death by

a Southern planter. When the facts were delivered by her two American students, she said that after all, the idea was the same. The older wisdom.

One of the duties of a Fulbright visitor was lecturing in other Italian towns. I was invited to lecture at the American Cultural Center in Genoa. Faulkner had died in July. I'd reread him for the first time since college and talked about him. Spiced with Italian reference (see below), the talk was considered a success, and the professor of English at the University of Genoa, who'd refused to invite previous Fulbright lecturers, asked the Fulbright Office to have me speak to his students. He wanted a survey of American literature since 1945. Clearly a talk one couldn't prepare. Anyway, I'd understood it was to be a seminar for a few graduate students. We could just "fire on the breeze" as one of my Venetian students put it. In Genoa, there were posters with my name and the subject plastered on public announcement boards. I was driven to an enormous lecture room and found six hundred faces waiting to be stuffed. I'd been a professional teacher for thirteen years, but was no good at public speeches. Not, at any rate, impromptu ones. Terror leans on syntax. Sentences mazier than Henry James's clunked out in the great aula. *The audience, once so bright and open, closed, clouded. (The professor was delighted: another American failure.)*

The talk was given November 22, 1962, one year to the day before President Kennedy's assassination. I couple the events because I think Kennedy belongs more to the group of great charmers who died during his administration, Hemingway, Faulkner, Marilyn Monroe, than to the victims of 1968. All these deaths made for a kind of dusk of individuality.

It's no accident that Hemingway's name appears—mis-spelled—in the diaries of Lee Harvey Oswald and Arthur Bremer, the dark side of the Individuality moon. The en-chanting loner, the heroic skeptic, who made his own system of restraints* imposed itself on almost every schoolboy of the forties and fifties: to have experience and to record it finely, to contrive a natural, yet exciting, public personality, this meant almost everything.

Faulkner's impassioned public shyness became a glam-orous public fact. When the Kennedys invited him to the White House, everyone in the country knew that he said it was pretty far to travel for a hamburger.

The next phalanx of literary celebrities look like old carbons: Salinger, the Hermit-Saint, and Mailer, the Per-former. Deeply serious and gifted, in "the dark glass of the media," they look like neurotic caricatures of Faulkner and Hemingway.

FAULKNER is a name known to all literate people in Italy. Indeed, Faulkner was written about here almost as early as he was written about in his own country: Cesare Pavese's famous review of *Sanctuary* was published in *La Cultura* in April 1934, and although Pavese's opinion of Faulkner altered for the better, one can still read this early account of Faulkner's relationship to Sherwood Anderson and be pleased by how much Pavese noticed, even if one feels—as he later must have—that he did not notice enough.

When Faulkner died, Italian newspapers and magazines recorded the death with as much solemnity as anyone (I

---

* Hemingway's Catholicism was not a well-known public fact.

discount the necessitous rapacity of these hounds of print for stories). In *L'Espresso*, Paolo Milano recalled that Faulkner sported a Van Dyke beard and dressed like a dandy in the Hollywood of the thirties, thus detaching himself from the depression garb of most writers, the worker's tieless shirt and dark suit. That Faulkner should have been as conscious about clothes as, say, Baudelaire, may surprise Americans more than Italians. Many American students who know Faulkner through his work and through the literary underworld which brought accounts of his "cracker" habit of carrying a gallon jug of corn whiskey suspended by an index finger over his shoulder, his Garbo-shyness of interviewers, literary people, and the press, must have thought him a Neanderthal man, a literary accident, better reflected in the monstrosity of his unclassical English than in the emotional brilliance which that monstrosity expressed. Indeed, Pavese was of this school: "*Un angelo senza cura d'anime,*" he called Faulkner in 1934; and also: a man with magic narrative gifts but wild and morally neutral, a writer who registered actions without caring about them.

Now of course, almost all critics, Italian, English, Japanese, know that Faulkner was a most conscious artist, a man who, if fired by immense passions, nonetheless developed literary equipment to deal with them, who was much more conscious and self-conscious than those of us who criticize him because so much of his consciousness had to be—and was—reduced to narrative expression. The great passion which Faulkner's work suggests is not the passion which the inorganic tumult of a volcano might represent, but the passion which long concentration on loved and hated objects will yield. I suppose the best natural symbol for such passion is the incessant power of the sea. Such passion was sensed by Pavese long ago and described in such phrases as "*la lenta realtà*," and "*il tono trasognato*"; and it was that despite what Pavese called "*i piatti e faticosi monologhi interiori*" of *As I Lay Dying*. This passion was capable of making "*scoppiare una voce, un dialogo in un alto silenzio, in una tensione quasi di prodigio.*"

Faulkner's passion is one which slows up reality, though the slowness is not that of ennui, but of tension, of continuous and growing clarification as more and more is brought to bear on, say, a simple encounter, the past of a character rising around him mixed with his sense of the objects which now surround him. I remember being amazed at the tension of the early scene in *Light in August* in which one wonders simply whether Mrs. Armstid, that "gray woman, not plump and not thin, manhard, workhard, in a serviceable gray garment worn savage and brusque, her hands on her hips, her face like those of generals who have been defeated in battle" will consent to give the pregnant Lena breakfast. It takes almost as much time in the reading as it would in life, and in one sense you might say that it is not part of the *real story* of the novel. Yet just as the word *brusque* was never before used to describe the way a garment is worn and is still revealing, compelling, *right*, even as it outrages—or at least twits—one's sense of classical English rightness, so the long moment in which Mrs. Armstid decides to cook for Lena is right for the *real story*, that of acceptance and birth.

"*Lenta realtà.*" So much of our own life is passed in a fuzzy, undefined feeling-state that an encounter with the form of that fuzziness—the rise and fall of our feelings as they relate to the rest of our life and the lives of others, the collective lives of families and societies—is shocking, thrilling, beautiful. A month ago, in the Scrovegni Chapel in Padua, I was struck by the length, the space, the *"lenta realtà"* of the woman who is spinning while Saint Anne is on her knees receiving from the angel the news that she is to be Mary's mother. That right arm, stretched out along the invisible yarn the spool of which dangles from the hand, took as much time to paint as anything in the picture, especially as it is pictorially broken by a porch pillar. Is it part of the *real story* of the annunciation to Saint Anne? Of course. The "story" is that of the presence of the marvelous in the familiar, and the great, permanent gesture of weaving—itself a form of creation—is the human sign of participation in the miraculous.

Here in Italy, even in this most active Italian city, where every day that powerful "symbol" of continuity and passion brings novelty to your door, and whence, every day, you dispatch upon it what will bring renovation and discovery to others, even here, you are surrounded, as we in America are not so conspicuously surrounded, by the artifacts of patience and of genius, most of them assembled in times during which what Wordsworth called "the rapid communication of intelligence" did not break hourly upon artisans and artists, despoiling them of the concentration that works of considered passion demand.

Like Giotto, shut up for months in the small chapel which was his alone to fill, Faulkner, as much as he could, stayed away from the buzz of production and publicity which make a Calvary for a serious artist. He stayed close to home. Home was, of course, a place designed for the retreat which a man needs, especially after he has had—as Faulkner had—a period of time between his mastery of the familiar and his return to isolate himself from the unfamiliar. Faulkner in the South, in Oxford, Mississippi, was not so unlike Joyce in Trieste, Zurich, and Paris, shut up in a study, remembering and finding words for what was remembered, getting refreshed now and then by visitors from Dublin or letters from his aunts and friends; not so different from Giotto, in Padua, far from Tuscany, remembering perhaps a cousin's face as she spun yarn; or Dante in Padua or Verona or Ravenna, as, say, he remembered the "Bicci, *vocato* Forese" with whom he had exchanged joking *tenzone*, putting him into *Purgatorio* when he needed someone there for gluttony (perhaps in a vein of jovial nostalgia). Faulkner, exiled by the need for solitude, fuels his conception from the memory of the place which was not, as much as it was, the same place in which he wrote.

There are twenty-five books on Faulkner's roll, and perhaps half of them are great additions to all literate lives: *The Sound and the Fury, As I Lay Dying, The Hamlet, Light in August, The Town, Go Down Moses, Collected Stories, Sanctuary, The Wild Palms*, a few more. All these books have strong, almost classical narratives, though all —more or less like every work of the new fiction which Henry James and Conrad and Ford Madox Ford developed in the nineties and the early part of the twentieth century, and which Joyce and Proust brought to its greatest height in the teens and twenties of the century—have broken the conventional time scheme of narrative and fitted the temporal pieces together in accord with a more realistic style of recollection, a recollection shaped by passion under the pressure of narrative. Not content with this apparent destruction of the "natural happenings," Faulkner, like the other artists, particularly Proust and Joyce, rearranged his narrative in other "unnatural" ways: a story is told through four different minds, each allowed a session of fifty or sixty pages; or through ten minds, each allowed a series of interrupted sessions; or through a mind which is suddenly and frequently taken over, as it were, by another mind. So the natural world of fuzz-flow is carefully, consciously shaped, misshaped for the purpose of alienating, and then clarifying, outraging, and then thrilling familiar perception.

From the beginning of a Faulkner novel we are in the midst of a situation, and it may be pages before we can find out where. Sometimes the confusion is increased by the disorderliness of the report; it may take quite a time before we acknowledge the truth of a title and decide that the opening monologue of *The Sound and the Fury* is being "told by an idiot," though it does not signify "nothing." Listen to the opening paragraph of this great book:

> Through the fence, between the curling flower spaces, I could see them hitting. They were coming toward where the flag was and I went along the fence. Luster was hunting in the grass by the flower tree. They took the flag out, and they were hitting. Then they put the flag back and they went to the table, and he hit and the other hit. Then they went on, and I went along the fence. Luster came away from the flower tree and we went along the fence and they stopped and we stopped and I looked through the fence while Luster was hunting in the grass.
> "Here, caddie." He hit.

It will be some time before we know that it is Benjy, a thirty-three-year-old castrated idiot confusing the talk of the golfers asking the caddie for golf clubs and his own beloved sister Caddie. One asks why Faulkner needs to confuse the "real story" with such a narrator, and the answer is of course that the real story depends on Benjy's purity: the idiot is incapable of reporting things incorrectly even if he does not know that the flag is the marker of a golf hole and that the men on the course are not talking about his sister. In this whirligig of impression, we need a stable set of judgments. If these judgments are an idiot's, this is not without significance.

Faulkner's great stories transmit the delight of new ways of thinking and feeling associated with a special place and filled with special, now familiar, characters: wild thin-necked farmers, maddened by poverty; shrewd, omnipres-ent, almost omniscient sewing-machine salesmen; dis-placed romantics as sensitive as air, incapable of ordering their feelings about people or places; inexorable half-acre tycoons moving to the ownership of towns; demented cow-lovers; earth mothers, so lushly sexual that the most fanati-cal career can be disarranged by them; acid-hearted haters, maniacal and fatal; great women, enduring every hurt and injustice, triumphant no matter what their end. These and many more, all given names, homes, clothes, given *stories*, all as immediately identifiable as Hamlet or Francesca of Rimini, Madame Verdurin, Bloom, il Gattopardo or any of the thousand men and women whom we know better than we know ourselves or our fathers: Ratliff, Jason Compson, Flem Snopes, Eula Varner, Henry Armstid, Dilsey.

I must not let a foreign audience forget that Faulkner must be thought of as one of the world's great comic writ-ers, great in the sense that his comedy is not finished off with joke, anecdote, or peculiarity, but by pathos and trag-edy. There are comic scenes in Faulkner which, written from a slightly different point of view, would not stir a breath of laughter, and there are, as well, immensely mov-ing scenes which could become occasions for roars. Much of Faulkner is borderline, and can be read one way one time, one way another.

To refresh fatigued responses, to make much of little, little of much: it is an artistic mission. So when Faulkner died in July even many who had never read a line of his mourned that special mourning for the departure of unique makers. Perhaps it is not too much to say in a public address by a foreigner that the international reciprocity of which we think so much in political terms is achieved most naturally by such a man, who, even while turning his eye on his own narrow preserve of locale/time/self, releases the reverberant power of that "*lenta realtà*" which Pavese, thirty years ago, recognized as a magnificent export.

One sort of work that—properly—goes with the wind is the introduction. There are human beings whose finest moments are introductory. (Isn't the comedian Georgie Jessel remembered—if he is—as America's Toastmaster?) Now and then, one can say something that counts within the introductory minutes. My old friend Bruno Bettelheim, somewhat estranged from the local psychoanalytic community, asked me to introduce him at some gathering in the spring of 1976. It made me think about his extraordinary career and I talked for five or six minutes about it. The result was taped and a portion set up in type for a magazine. The magazine editor was cashiered, my piece disappeared, and what remained was what is printed here.

Introducing Bruno Bettelheim,
May 5, 1976

BRUNO BETTELHEIM'S WORK confirms that special relationship between the humanistic and scientific study of personality which was proclaimed forty years ago this very week. The occasion was the eightieth birthday celebration of Sigmund Freud in Vienna. The proclaimer was Thomas Mann. In his talk, Mann placed Freud in the tradition of Novalis, Kierkegaard, Schopenhauer, and Nietzsche, a tradition which wrenches psychological truths from a metaphysical pessimism which regards man as *das kranke Tier*, "the sick animal" who, in the words of Victor Hugo, "affirms himself by infirmity." Freud—said Mann—was also the herald of "a humanism of the future . . . bolder, freer, blither, productive of a riper art than any possible in our neurotic, fear-ridden, hate-ridden world."

Mann spoke from the lip of that world. Two years later, Freud, pried out of Vienna, was dying in London, and Bruno Bettelheim—who was in Mann's audience*—was in Dachau.

It is one of the pivotal episodes of modernity that Bruno Bettelheim survived that diabolical system, and survived it in part by understanding it. His description of his understanding came from the United States, which Freud, in one of his last letters (to Arnold Zweig), described as an "anti-Paradise," a "caricature of a country," but one "so roomy and full of possibility that it is said to ultimately please."

The way it pleased Bruno Bettelheim involved the expansion, refinement, and reinterpretation of Freud's own work. The environment of Freudian therapy is bare as a Beckett play, its time span as controlled as a classical one. The select hours of sympathetic audition to the patient on the couch could not serve the battered human beings whose sense of the world's inhospitality had made them "old prisoners" of their own Dachaus. These were the people—the children—whom Bruno Bettelheim was to heal. As if following the hint of his own name ("home for beggars") he created a home whose roominess, sense of possibility and almost unlimited time were to make them welcome in the world. "New types of architecture, a change of heart."

Here in Chicago, this city of great architecture, in the context of the great university, the "home for the heart" radiated that sense of salvage, optimism, and rigorous, enlightened pragmatism which flows from the notion that en-

* He told me that Freud wasn't.

vironment and personality, activity and meaning are fused. This Bettelheim credo characterizes much fine work that comes from this city and this university. What we may call the Chicago realism of Fermi and Friedman, Gottschalk, Geertz, Levi, and Crane, of Jane Addams, Harriet Monroe, and Louis Sullivan, of Boorstin, Bellow, and Bettelheim, makes as beautiful a story as that fine tale from the twentieth-century Vienna woods sung by Freud and Wittgenstein, Loos, Musil, Broch, Webern, Berg, Mahler, and Schönberg.

The following "portraits" are the equivalents of those distorted miniatures which virtuoso painters enjoyed putting onto polished spheres or other mirrored surfaces of the canvas. They come at the sitter through other portraits, biographical or autobiographical, and are as much about the act of representation as those represented.

That Devilish, Thinning Art

THE FOURTH VOLUME of Edel's biography* ended with James's new face. For the new century, he had shaved off his beard. Fifty-seven, he felt forty. He'd worked through his failure in the theater, written a series of novels about abused children which—Edel's view—released him from the delicate shackles of the James family and from an old fear of erotic love, and he had come as close to this as he ever would. Now, in the fifth volume, the massive little man, ensconced with five servants and a secretary-typist in his Rye home, respectful colleagues (Conrad, Wells, Crane, Ford) within easy—sometimes too easy—reach, keeps fit with bicycle rides and prepares to write the three densely refined novels of love's discovery, renunciation, and acceptance. In 1904, after twenty-one years away, he returns to America, lectures on "the lesson of Balzac" to amazed audiences from Philadelphia to Los Angeles, and writes his

---

*Leon Edel, *Henry James: The Master (1901–1916)* (New York: Lippincott, 1972). All five volumes have been condensed and touched up for the edition which Edel wants preserved. A sprightly, large-minded gentleman, Edel acknowledges (at least in person) his gratitude to such severe criticism as this. I have not checked the new edition for alterations and repairs.

brilliant analytic evocation of *The American Scene*; he works out his literary monument, the Balzacian New York edition, suffers its financial failure, and then, just after becoming an English citizen, dies in the middle of that "horrible, unspeakable, iniquitous" war which undid the society he had rendered and subtilized. On his death bed, mind peeling, James had dedicated two coherent letters about the splendor of his plans, one of which he'd signed "Napoleone," the other with his own name. In Edel's view, he had long shared the Corsican's glory-hunger. (Oddly enough, the physical resemblance—at least in the death masks—is remarkable.

For the twenty-one years he has devoted to this biography, Edel has worked against James's detestation of that "devilish" and "thinning" art of biography which "simplifies even while seeking to enrich." Hoping to control his biographic future, James had burned a mountain of papers. What counted for the higher consciousness did not exist as a man, only as "the monster and magician of a thousand masks . . . so generalised, so consummate and typical, so frankly amused with himself, that is with his art, with his power, with his theme, that it is as if he came to meet us more than his usual half-way." Such an illusion-dispensing monster cannot fool a biographer. An Edel will dig up another monster, the James whose flirtatiousness may have led Constance Woolson to kill herself, who, annoyed at a rutting cat, killed it with a stick, who fell in love with Hugh Walpole, and who (according to Maugham in volume 4 and Spender in volume 5) turned down his gallant offer with "I can't. I can't."

The romantic artist has been famously hungry for attention and famously jealous of his privacy. The romantic biographer is professionally inured to his subject's desires and scientifically prepared to foil them. His biographic equipment sometimes includes self-deprecating humor. I once heard Edel recall a dream in which James reproached him for claiming that he—James—owned a certain piece of furniture. "You're wrong," refuted the dreaming biographer and flourished the oneiric receipt.

Edel needs more than receipts. James's warning about the biographic menace to an artist's work forces his biographer to include self-defense. "James was prepared to accept the art of biography if it became a 'quest of imaginative experience.'" But an artist's "imaginative experience" either exists in his work, or is beyond transcription. The biographer's choice is to isolate characteristics, call them "figures in the carpet," and thus shrink the work toward its own skeleton; or, to do what James tried in his own biographies, an artistic recreation, a portrait. Aware of this, Edel invites his critics (in the preface to this last volume) to consider his own artistry; it is only "proper for artists to write about artists."

A perilous invitation. But serious, and worth a look. Here is the would-be artist Edel typically at work introducing a chapter on James's most famous typist: "When Theodora Bosanquet went that summer's day in 1907 to Miss Petherbridge's secretarial office, an employment agency, she had no notion that this would be one of the most eventful days of her life. She felt somewhat slack and headachey. She was disinclined to brave the noise of the tube, and took a bus to Conduit Street."

This is not quite "The summer evening had begun to fold the world in its mysterious embrace," but close enough to make one sniff unintended burlesque. (If "that sum-

mer's day," "disinclined," and "headachey" are Miss Bosanquet's words, let's have the quotation marks.) Miss
Bosanquet's "diary of that August gives us a distinct picture": James's "grimy gardener" takes her luggage, she set-
tles in, takes dictation, keeps her journal, and becomes "increasingly worshipful of the Master, yet it was not blind
worship. She retained a strong sense of her own identity."
Edel summarizes the identity: "She was a true hand-maid-
en of the Master."

In a long work, so much of which must be tied to docu-
mentation, insipidity of this sort may signal the biographer's relief at a moment of freedom. There's too much of
it: James urges his brother to let his son stay in Paris, and
Edel's contribution is, "Henry James was thinking of his
own art-starved condition in Cambridge forty years earlier." So it goes.

Then there is the Edelian prose with its coy allusiveness
(Edith Wharton discovering "new realities within the house
of mirth") and poesy ("the latter in a letter"; "the pom-
pously-embanked river"). Like many apparently faithful
servants, Edel robs the Master's larder; his moustache is
smeared with Jamesian jam.

Yet, yet. Not a work of high art, but somehow a moving
biography. The long volumes give a sense of James's days
and evenings, of the years as James slows down, shuffles off
his social armour, deepens and strengthens. Like many
remarkable men, James evoked a responsive intelligence
from those who talked to or about him. Conrad, Wells,
Shaw and Edith Wharton spar with or describe him brilliantly. Even Edel rises on occasion to a spare analysis of a
novel or situation.

The initial question in his biography was, Did nothing
happen to Henry James except the writing of an extremely

long shelf of books? In my view,* James lived a good deal more intensely than most of us burgher adventurers; that is, if living be depth of feeling, comprehension, sympathy, and range of expression. James was a wonderful friend who elicited strength and a sense of beauty and possibility from nearly all who knew him, and at an age when most turn into sentimental curmudgeons, he learned, worked, and felt at the top of his powers.

No Boswell, Edel has discovered and assembled most of James's life stuff. I suppose he is James's ideal biographer: his assiduity is reined by a banality which preserves what James wanted to preserve, the irreducibility of his work.

---

* Not that of the bear of Literary Commonsense, the late Philip Rahv (cf. his *New York Review of Books* review of volume 5, February 10, 1972).

Self-Invention

THE YEAR Franklin Roosevelt became president, Mark Harris became a writer. Age eleven, he began a diary in which he has written almost every day since. A year or two later, he became a novelist. The novel was epistolary, like the marvelous comedy he published a quarter of a century later, *Wake up, Stupid*. The audience was small, however, consisting of his friend and rival, Norman Apell. To Apell, Harris wrote from summer camp about an "Inter-Camp Baseball League in which boys in the most elegant uniforms travelled around like professionals. Each camp," Harris wrote Apell "was required to maintain a perfectly barbered diamond and sparkling dressing-rooms. . . . The grandstands were spacious, girls pressed forward for our autographs—how boring to be giving out my autograph all day. . . . Some people might find this sort of thing exciting, but I'd much rather be at home with *him* all summer on the good old baking streets and good old rocky dust-choked sandlots of Mount Vernon." Harris conjured up the stands, the diamonds, and the girls of Rochester, Utica, and Troy. "My letters were mailed by the most careful calculation, bearing in mind our eight day swing through Schenectady, complicated by the tedious necessity of coming back through Albany to make up a washed-out game." The twelve-year-old liar checked out calendars, weather reports, maps—"for useful details"—so, in Ogdensburg, he "picked up some Canadian money, in Lockport some of the kids went to see Niagara Falls falling, but I stayed in the hotel resting my pulled muscle. I had never been to Ogdensburg, never been to Lockport, never pulled a mus-

cle. Where I *was* was on my cot at Rest Hour at Camp
Secor on my way to becoming a novelist."

Harris published his ninth—official—novel, *Killing Everybody*, in 1973, the same year he did the screenplay for
his best-known book, *Bang the Drum Slowly*. For ten years
though, he had been publishing installments of autobiography—*Twentyone Twice*, *Mark the Glove Boy; or, The
Last Days of Richard Nixon**—and not many people took
notice of them. Which was a mistake.

There are all sorts of autobiographers (the scholar Misch
treats thousands going back millennia). There are Cellinis
and Casanovas whose manic flamboyance fills the darker
quarters of old age, self-deprecating explainers like Henry
Adams, nostalgic lyricists, nostalgic documentarians, philosophers who condense their lives into historical exempla.
Modern autobiography, an account of a life interesting not
because it is the life of a king or an adventurer but because
it is a human story, is usually dated from Rousseau's *Con-
fessions*, which appeared posthumously in 1782. Now almost everyone who can write or read thinks his life story is
worth publishing.

Fiction writers are often fiction writers to disguise their
lives, or to express impulses which would jail them if they
substituted revolver for typewriter. Part of the delight of
Mark Harris's new autobiography† is his analysis of the
way his novels express, disguise, amplify, alter, and substitute for his own experience. Another pleasure here is
seeing how Harris's gift for storytelling makes novels whose
deepest connection with his experience is their having been

---

* The latest installment is a very funny, Boswellian biography, *Saul Bellow, Drum-
lin Woodchuck* (Athens: University of Georgia Press, 1980).
† *Best Father Ever Invented: The Autobiography of Mark Harris* (New York: Dial
Press, 1976).

written. The distinction between self-revelation and self-invention is subtle; in *Best Father Ever Invented* it is made as clearly as you're likely to see.

Much of the great charm of Harris's writing is that it feels so honest. Harris is able to keep one step ahead of his innocence, yet continue to shed more layers of innocence. He is an innocent by confession, not expression. By making verbal what most of us pass over in silence, afraid of others thinking us stupid, clumsy, banal, vicious, Harris somehow invents a man who seems not to be inventing, but merely coping with the world. Harris is always being tipped off, educated, shown the way. *All* he does is persist and react. And write. Oddly enough, these are enough to put him into the middle of all sorts of dramas: military dramas, hiring-and-firing dramas, dramas of paternity, friendship, profession, existential dramas involving not kingdoms but cigarette-smoking or job-hunting. The biggest drama is the Harris strip show. In front of your eyes, Harris strips and strips. Is it for real? Seldom will you read a book in which it seems so real. Such seeming appears to be the easiest literary job and is damn near the hardest. "Nothing so much prevents our being natural as the desire to seem so" (La Rochefoucauld). Harris pulls it off. He is able to sound both natural and unique for two reasons: one, he has been a writer for so many years that the unnatural act of turning one's thoughts and sensations into words is less unnatural for him than for 99.9 percent of the race, and two, Harris will not let either himself or the world alone. That is, he puts constant pressure on what he is, what he does, and what he thinks. There is an obligation to that diary. "Every day I must make an account." The autobiographical account involves weakness more than strength (though Harris is much too wise to duck his strength); it is the classic *Huck Finn* (though not the Mark Twain) route. Five pages in, and the sting is removed from Harris's vanity, hypocrisy, and egoism. The writer's charm has paid in advance for his damage. Harris becomes a good man before your eyes, and when this happens, everything that happens to him is interesting: his income, his jobs, what he eats, what he weighs, going AWOL, getting fired, driving back and forth across the country, living in Hiroshima, giving up cigarettes, breaking his daughter's nose, teaching, reading, writing a dissertation, a play, this book. En route are his instructors and opponents (often the same) who are presented clearly, but in the clarity of their meaning for Harris. There must be thirty remarkable people in this book, presented with a rapid power very few writers could manage: parents, children, agents, soldiers, publishers, deans, some celebrities (Hayakawa, Alfred Knopf, Thornton Wilder, Walter Clark) but all now in equal celebrity because of Harris's portraiture. (The slightest, yet most beautiful portrait is of Harris's wife, Jo. This marriage may be put in a museum.)

Harris's five-year-old son—"perhaps extorting, bribing me"—tells him one day he is "the best father ever invented." What you have in this book is the best Mark Harris yet invented, someone shuttled between his genes and his books, his teachers and his antagonists, what he does and what he reads, between the camp boy exciting the envy of Norman Apell and the autobiographer who ends the book with "When I completed my autobiography, I'd be the envy of my friends."

Malraux and de Gaulle

Ah, what a dreadful sound they make in the waning light,
The oaks being felled for Hercules' pyre!

VICTOR HUGO

DECEMBER 11, 1969, a Thursday. The snow falls on the isolated park behind Charles de Gaulle's house in the low Merovingian hills where-perhaps-Vercingetorix lost the crucial Gallic battle to Julius Caesar. De Gaulle's old minister, companion, and intellectual conscience, André Malraux, drives out from Paris, and the two men spend the day talking. The conversation and the scene are reconstructed by Malraux for their place in the second volume of his *Anti-memoirs*, but after de Gaulle's death, correcting proof, he sees that they make an independent book. "My reasons for publishing now these fragments . . . will be clear to anyone who reads them."

Clearer, perhaps, than Malraux thought. *Felled Oaks* (*Les chênes qu'on abat*) is a remarkable, disagreeable, profound, un- and re-settling book. Out of it comes a de Gaulle simply grand, accurate, humanly modest, assured, puzzled, and as deeply serene as any well-recorded man of history I know or can recall. Beside him, interrupting, flattering, provoking, interpreting, and misinterpreting him, the self-proclaimed "great artist," who either allows us to see him as a buzzing intellectual or believes he emerges as the proper reflector-creator of his truly loved friend and leader.

"Free man is not envious; he willingly accepts what is

great and rejoices it can exist," Malraux quotes from Hegel, and, surely, he thought he published this fragment in order to recall France and the world to the greatness de Gaulle wrenched out of *her* (and which de Gaulle incarnated).

What is talked over here is mostly remarkable. There is, as well, repetition; there is also the irrepressible intrusion of Malraux's memory-fragments cohering only about the insecure ego of a brilliant man who was never able to make moving sense or beauty out of them; and, finally, there is what will last here, the iron simplicity, wisdom, and decency of what had before seemed de Gaulle's almost-mad pomposity.

The talk is about history, historical action, the images and models people draw from clouds, cats, butterflies and great works, about France, despotism, civilization, women, Napoleon, the end of Europe, the use and uselessness of endeavor. De Gaulle's remarks are in boldface, Malraux's talk and speculation in ordinary print. This is graphic propriety. Again and again, de Gaulle brings intelligence out of Malraux clouds:

MALRAUX: And if our civilization is certainly not the first to deny the immortality of the soul, it is the first in which the soul has no importance. . . .

DE GAULLE: Why do you speak as if you were a believer, since you are not?

MALRAUX: Renan was not a fool. . . .

DE GAULLE: That depends on the day.

And:

MALRAUX: Athens was crushed by Sparta with no great effect on its art. . . . But it would all have ended with Alexander anyhow. . . .

DE GAULLE: Yes. And at dawn, the wolf ate Monsieur Seguin's goat, which had fought it off all night.

The difference between a great artist and a great man of action, even when the medium for both is words, is that the great artist makes what counts for him on his own schedule, but the man of action has to respond immediately to what's given, or, at least, has to create the occasion at the right time. Even if Malraux were a great artist—which he has never been, even in *La condition humaine*—he would probably suffer in an unrevised exchange. (Though Malraux "reconstructed" this "non-interview," he was surely true to de Gaulle; and will escape *his idea of himself*.)

De Gaulle is aware of the difference between writing and talk: "How odd it is that a man has to drive himself so hard, to tear out of himself what he wants to write! Yet it is almost easy to draw out what one wants to say in speech." Malraux intersperses the December talk with great lines from de Gaulle speech "occasions": "These realists who know nothing of reality . . . Vichy, which holds France by the wrists while the enemy cuts her throat . . . Those who claimed to govern our country open their mouths only to order her to roll in the mud."

There is another surprise in *Felled Oaks*. It turns out that de Gaulle is more a man of words than Malraux, Malraux more a poet-in-action than a creator of beautiful works. (I'd guess de Gaulle admired his famous courage more than his famous intellect.)

Malraux was on the move for fifty years, all over the world, hunting artistic, personal and political excitement, and responding to it with fearlessness, ingenuity, and his sense of heroism. He is the polyperformer for whom vast learning and many books are but the ash of heroic activity.

Yet these are what he leaves behind.* (The Paris monuments, cleaned when he was de Gaulle's minister of culture, blacken each day.)

De Gaulle too will pass away, at least on the time scale of oaks and butterflies (or even Aeschylus) of which they talk so often. But Malraux, a nonbeliever, hungered for historic permanence. His book on de Gaulle, the finest record available of the great man, was his way of hitching to a more fixed star than any in his life with the exception of Mao Tse-tung (whose portrait is the gem of the *Antimemoir*). This is the clear publication reason which flowed under the ice of this commemoration.

What one carries away of de Gaulle is the man who thinks of himself as a kind of Tintin (the dear innocent of the French comic books), as Don Quixote, and as the old man in Hemingway's book who drags home a skeleton fish. ("It depends on the day.")

De Gaulle, playing with his cat, twitted by his slyly charming wife—another surprise—remembering his beloved, feeble-minded daughter, recalling Stalin's fierce grip on his leg every time a German was killed in the film they watched, speculating on Jackie Kennedy's future ("I thought she'd marry Sartre or you"), this immense old fellow with a Cyrano nose (he liked Cyrano) personally, singly, uniquely revived the greatness of a country, elevated the politics of almost every man he met (although Lyndon Johnson "never seemed to take the trouble to think") and left behind in this important if unbeautiful book, a print of himself which I think offers human beings a new and surprising model of personal grandeur.

* Malraux said he wanted to be remembered as a writer "and not a writer, *hélas*, but a writer without the *hélas* and without the exclamation point." See *Lazarus* (New York: Holt, Rinehart and Winston, 1977).

Sulzberger and Beckett:
Sketch for a Diptych

REVIEWING one of C. L. Sulzberger's volumes of memoir* several years ago, C. P. Snow discussed the "great American political commentators" who have had "more influence than almost any politician: if one looks beneath the trappings of office, they have often had more power. They have had entrée to public figures all over the world and have seen them more intimately than any politician could. . . . Among those active in the world's affairs, they have been the freest men alive."

There's something to add to Snow's account when considering Sulzberger's work, either his column† or his volumes of memoir. It has to do with the way important men talked to him. When they did, they put on their intellectual coats and ties. They seemed to know that their strategies, sympathies, and intentions were under the fire of international examination. It didn't mean that a general, ministerial secretary, senator, king or premier who talked to Sulzberger did not try to use him, knowing that his column had

---

* The four volumes are: *A Long Row of Candles* (New York: Macmillan, 1969), *The Last of the Giants* (New York: Macmillan, 1970), *An Age of Mediocrity* (New York: Macmillan, 1973), and *Postscript with a Chinese Accent* (New York: Macmillan, 1974). A selection from the four volumes, *Seven Continents and Forty Years* (New York: Quadrangle/New York Times Book Co., 1977), despite a handsome preface by a "fellow-adventurer," André Malraux, slights the cumulative power of the thick originals.

† His last column appeared on January 1, 1978. He was obliged to retire at sixty-five, a *Times* regulation which had not (been) applied to James Reston, three years Sulzberger's senior.

become a kind of unofficial international agenda. World leaders knew that his experience was so wide and his files so detailed that it was not easy to pull diplomatic wool over his eyes. If action repudiated statement, that repudiation made the political and moral record of the repudiator. The column was then not only a sort of world seminar, it served to check one of the endemic vices of leadership, mendacity.

Again more in the memoirs than in the columns, the sense of international policies is depicted with the incidental but crucial (as well as charming) details of expression, gesture, occasion, and place. The public pronouncements of public men seldom nourish hungry mentality. Yet the same men whose speeches and press conferences were foul with bromides show up in Sulzberger's pages as men and women of fascinating opinions, tastes, habits, and stories. Like a greater memoirist, the duc de Saint-Simon, Sulzberger wanted to convey the life behind the opinions. Since he is a man of strong feelings and intelligence as well as one alert to tone and gesture, his memoirs are filled with marvelous human portraits.

I came across the memoirs a couple of years ago, as I was finishing a novel about a journalist. Although the fictional journalist was intended to serve the story in which he functioned more than actuality, I did read fifty or so volumes of memoirs in order to pillage detail. Most of the memoirs were little more than anecdotal piles rough-hewn by the reflective banality. The Sulzberger memoirs, "loose, baggy monsters" though they were, exuded intellectual power. And they circled the heart of international life. I stole what my style could accommodate, finished the book, then wrote a confession and fan letter to their author. In July 1977, we had a wonderful four-hour luncheon in one of his splendid Paris hangouts. (La Boule d'Or? Perhaps. I do remember the iced *framboise* drinks, the salmon, the wine, Sulzberger's cocker, Christopher, feasting silently under the table, and the easy pleasure of the talk.)

Two days earlier, I'd spent a few hours with another remarkable man I'd met for the first time, Samuel Beckett. I thought I'd do a double portrait: one would be of a man who'd spent forty-odd years reporting the world *out there*, the other a man who'd spent the same time inventing a world from inside.

It turned out that Beckett and Sulzberger made an interesting diptych. Each was a native English speaker from the English periphery (Ireland, the United States) who'd spent most of his adult life in Paris. Both were excellent linguists, both men of conspicuous intellectual and physical energy. They even had similar grizzled, blue-eyed looks (though Beckett's face is gaunt, his eyes huge). Neither is concerned much with appearance (except, perhaps, negatively). Beckett dresses like an urchin and carries a Woolworth-style briefcase.† Sulzberger paid more for clothes, and there was a blue scheme, though it looked as if it had been worked out numerically.

Finally, I don't believe that either man knew the degree of his own importance (though Sulzberger had been accused of excessive self-absorption). For Beckett, the great literary figure was Joyce, and he would not bear a hint that his own work had anything like the same order of power. Yet when we talked of Joyce's impulse to give up writing,

---

† In September 1979 Beckett looked spiffy in tweed jacket and oyster-colored turtleneck. His face was less gaunt, and his eyes, recovered from a cataract operation, were softer, more rested in crinkled sockets. For more of this other view, see "The Invention of the Real," in this volume.

Beckett said Joyce might have "made a fine career" as a singer, "like Fischer-Dieskau." Beckett's modesty about both himself and literature itself (though one feels he'd die for a sentence) was not in the least literary or theatrical. It belonged to a human economy that was not the product of exhaustion—as one had heard—but choice.

Sulzberger felt that he had never affected policy (except for his World War II reports on Yugoslavian factions). He did not regard himself as a thinker, only as a tenacious and systematic reporter. Nine months a year for forty years he'd whirled around the earth. The logistics of travel and communications were intricate; his life was organized about them.

As it was about a wonderful wife, Marina Lada of Chios and Athens, who was said to have had "neither enemy nor acquaintance." She died unexpectedly after a minor operation in the summer of 1976. That day, Sulzberger walked to his office from the hospital and banged out his 725-word column:

> There is a particular sadness in the fact that China, which had devoted such special attention to the problem of predicting earthquakes and preparing threatened areas to minimize casualties, should just now have suffered the most terrible shock anywhere on earth during the past twelve years.

The column ended:

> The human animal is a curious beast given to bloody quarrels over politics, religion, ideology or that relic of the territorial imperative called nationalism. But tragedy has a temporary way of transcending such follies. One can only hope more fortunate countries will extend to China at this moment the help-

ing hand it assuredly needs, although it is perhaps too proud to say so.

This column objectifies personal feeling as inconspicuously as *Samson Agonistes* objectified the blind, woman-weakened Milton's condition. It is a tribute to the artistry of a few good journalists glued to—but not denatured by—the world out there.

Beckett's work, almost entirely severed from that world, is an addition to it; a new mental color. In the little bar near the Luxembourg gardens, Beckett said that the only time he'd otherwise participated in the world's affairs was when the Nazis began killing his friends. He joined an underground network: his job, condensing intelligence reports so that, photographed, they could be fitted into matchboxes. ("Reality favors symmetries," wrote Borges, another modern master of the laser and the remnant.)

No one will claim that Sulzberger's work—reportorial, fictional, or historical—constitutes the same sort of addition to the world's mind as Beckett's. Still, that double gift of provoking and recording the significant and amusing talk of an immense variety of people makes Sulzberger part of an even more elite group than the one C. P. Snow described, that of the first-rate memoirists (Walpole, Grimm, Saint-Simon, Boswell) whose record of their times is the caviar of documentary literature.

Moving of the Earth

Since nothing hinders the mobility of the
Earth, I think we should now see whether
more than one movement belongs to it.

COPERNICUS,
On the Revolutions of Heavenly Spheres

Cleon . . . the most violent man in Athens
. . . spoke as follows:—"I have often been
convinced that a democracy is incapable of
empire . . . obedience is insured not by sui-
cidal concessions, but by the superiority of
one's own strength . . . if, right or wrong,
you determine to rule, you must carry out
your principles and punish the Mytilenians
. . . or else you must give up your empire
and cultivate honesty without danger."

THUCYDIDES,
The Peloponnesian War

"Oh, Jake," Brett said, "we could have had
such a damned good time together."
Ahead was a mounted policeman in khaki
directing traffic. He raised his baton. The
car slowed suddenly pressing Brett against
me.
"Yes," I said. "Isn't it pretty to think so?"

HEMINGWAY,
The Sun Also Rises

This section has to do with "the great public world." Or, at least, with what a nosy, armchair intriguer like myself can make of it. The only piece which actually removed me from the armchair and put me on a plane was the one about the Carter White House ("Off the Sleeve"). A word from this armchair about Foreign Policy. It begins, I sup- pose, as official expression of commercial and intellectual interests. That is, it exists to make international business and travel easy. Somewhere along the line, official interest becomes interest in itself. Every action, cultural or belli- cose, intellectual or commercial, becomes important for policy makers. In the spirit of Jonson's Sir Politic Wouldbe (in Volpone*), the erotic, the culinary, the oneiric become signs of malevolent intention. Jonson's mad amateur of intelligence is the professional of the 1950s. (They were around in Jonson's day as well. The Venetian spy service was pretty fair.) In our time, we've seen idiotic nations. (*Idios. *Greek for a private person, one who does not take part in public concerns.) The official idiot is no longer a contradiction. President Nixon's taped comments on his agents were variations of Ben Jonson.*

PEREGRINE:

I have heard, sir,
That your baboons were spies, and that they were
A kind of subtle nation near to China.

SIR POLITIC WOULDBE:
Ay, ay, your Mamaluchi. Faith, they had
Their hand in a French plot or two; but they
Were so extremely given to women, as
They made discovery of all.
. . . .

SIR POLITIC WOULDBE:
He has received weekly intelligence,
Upon my knowledge out of the Low Countries
For all parts of the world, in cabbages;
And those dispensed again t'ambassadors,
In oranges, muskmelons, apricots . . .

(Whittaker Chambers' fruit of concealment was the pumpkin.)
Sir Politic also gives us the ancestry of modern statesmen. He's telling Peregrine about mountebanks, snake oil men and quacks:

They are the only knowing men of Europe:
Great general scholars, excellent physicians,
Most admired statesmen, professed favorites,
And cabinet counsellors to the greatest princes:

When the protective shell of Foreign Policy grows so heavy that the animal can hardly move, we arrive at the era of Henry Kissinger and Andrei Gromyko. (The American eagle, grounded, turns tortoise.) Kissinger's massive book is the great text of "tortoisery." Its weightiness is pumped with enough comedy to show us that in a lighter—less open—era, Kissinger could have written a more Cimarosan, if not Mozartian, memoir, something in the manner of his hero Bismarck's Errinerung und Gedächtnis. As it is, the best review of it would be Ogden Nash's

I think it clever of the turtle
In such a fix to be so fertile.

Fundamentals, Symmetries, and the Germans
April 30, 1973

WERNER HEISENBERG is soft of outline, plump, not fat, bald, the large head speckled, edged with white. His eyes have the radiant blue of high intelligence, they dominate a character-actor's face, full of expression from rapid command to a deprecation that bespeaks a conscientious—a learned—modesty. In a hall bulging in every aisle and through every door with students and faculty, he spoke in Chicago the afternoon of April 30 while, across the country in Washington, the chancellor of his country spent his first American day fishing in Chesapeake Bay because Washington was embroiled in the affairs of those descendants of other Germans, Haldeman, Ehrlichman, and Kleindienst. While these German derivatives were resigning and being rebuked for moral slither, Professor Heisenberg (who'd had his own wrestle with the exacting demons of public morality a quarter of a century before*) talked of the dilemmas modern physics faced because its language and logic had been designed for an outmoded "classical physics." Notions of velocity, force, position, and situations had brought discomfort to even such masters of the new as Bohr, Schrödinger, and Einstein. Their discomfort at such things as transition states and the uncertainty principle was equivalent to the contemporary obsession with fundamental particles, a search made futile by the "most

---

* His claim (in *Physics and Beyond*) is that he stayed in Germany to inhibit the manufacture of atomic weapons.

revolutionary discovery of the century," Dirac's forty-five-year-old description of the then-undiscovered positron. Every "fundamental" particle could be a configuration of many pair-bonds of material and antimaterial particles. What counted now was the investigation of such fundamental symmetries as isotopic spin and time conjugation.

This account of physical reality, a refined descendant of the Kantian critiques, oddly enough found an enfeebled sibling in the Washington section of the day: Mr. Ehrlichman's letter of resignation to President Nixon noted that "one of the toughest problems we have in this life is in seeing the difference between the apparent and the real, and in basing our actions only on that which is real."

As the unapprehended pair-bonds of the Heisenberg world-view could be apprehended only under bombardment, so the moral universe of the Washington Germans had come to light only under an investigatory bombardment spurred by hatred of the "Berlin Wall" the "German Mafia" had put up around the President. Haldeman was particularly detested. An old ad man, he'd promoted Purity—or its appearance—for J. Walter Thompson (his accounts were shaving creams, insecticides, waxes). Nondrinking, nonsmoking, a nonrecognizer of disease (like Ehrlichman, he's a Christian Scientist), Haldeman had kept the dirty flow of oddity away from the Boss's desk. "The narrow German always felt endangered, denationalized, by information which exposed him to the relativity and diversity of cultural values."[†]

Further apart than the languages of classical and modern physics were those of Mr. Nixon's foreign policy (de-

---

[†]Erik H. Erikson, *Childhood and Society* (New York: W. W. Norton, 1951), p. 311.

vised by his resident Heisenberg, Henry Kissinger) and his Watergate speech that evening. The vocabulary of his foreign policy is that of an elementary physics text: "multipolarity" and "shifting equilibria"[‡] describe the formidable arrangements Kissinger and Nixon hope will keep the world pacified. The fundamental symmetry aimed at is the old balance of power conjugated for our time by shifting interests and compensations. In any case, it is a language of contemporary reality, unlike the cornball rhetoric of Mr. Nixon's evening prayer-meeting exhortation before his iconography of authenticity (a bust of Lincoln, a picture of Pat, Julie, and Tricia, and American flags in his lapel and by the wall). Is it in part the strain of such disjunct vocabularies which accounts for the President's notorious television manner, the out-of-nowhere smiles scarring and disappearing on his face with the rapidity of particle tracks in a cloud chamber, the bobbled words, the hands folding toward prayer then shifting to a wrist-clasp? The *sincerity* is not simply false; its reality is so mixed up with the knowledge that it had to be *projected* that it almost always looks "caught in the act."

Mr. Nixon's Oedipal "search for the culprits" may be as irrelevant as the "search for the quark." The fundamental question is not who burgled, who bribed, who covered up, but the Heisenbergian question: what is the moral economy (fundamental symmetry) which made such actions likely? Heisenberg had been launched into the chartless waters of Uncertainty Principle by Einstein's remark, "It is theory which decides what we can observe." The world of Nixon and his "narrow Germans" seemed to spin on a

[‡] Cf. Henry Brandon, *The Retreat of American Power* (New York: Doubleday, 1973).

variation of that maxim: "Our version of rectitude decides what is right." According to Heisenberg, Einstein's maxim was intended as a description of what really happens; the smell of the Washington version came from its use as prescription and justification.

The Nixinger Doctrine

*H*ENRY BRANDON makes me feel like an insider. A newspaperman, Brandon is "the dean of Washington correspondents." Intelligence, sympathetic discretion and—undoubtedly—personal charm have made him the privileged recipient of inside dope on both sides of the Atlantic.

The men who shape and shake the planet apparently not only need but trust him; that is, as far as any public figure can trust any man whose livelihood depends on him and on whom he—often resentfully—depends.

Brandon's *The Retreat of American Power* is a critical exposition of the foreign policy Henry Kissinger devised along Richard Nixon's emotional and intellectual lines of force. After reading it, this old despiser of Richard Nixon was converted into a reluctant admirer. Walking officeward on Fifty-seventh Street to write a review, I was feeling that Mr. Nixon was a great international gamesman.

Two blocks from the Ray School, a ten-year-old boy walked my way. His milk-chocolate face was tense. Late for school? Forgotten his homework? Fight with his sister? Full of Nixon, Kissinger, Peking, Moscow, MIRVs and Suez, I somehow wanted to make connection between them and that worried boy. Instantly—sentimentally?—my mind traced the boy's tension to home misery, to ghetto misery, and that to such Brandoned events as the "high price" (the B-1 bomber) Nixon paid to get the "cooperation" of the Joint Chiefs of Staff in the strategic arms limitation talks.

All right, Nixon and Kissinger were, in a way, working for this boy. From that ethereal summit, they did sight a "generation of peace" which might, eventually, get money into that ghetto, if not a smile on that face. Cambodia, the "Pakistan tilt," the grinding of Indochina were, for them, slivers of a great design, their Doctrine of Multipolarity and Shifting Equilibria. For them, it made sense; and, after Brandon, it made sense to me.

"The trouble with war is that there's always one general who's wrong," Kissinger told Brandon. Despite the magnificent preparations, the careful position papers, the sifted options, there is always the gremlin of disaster. You minimized its presence (analyzed your opponents, counted your aces, swapped, compromised, held fast when necessary, yielded strategically) but there it was, the original sin of the world's body. The tragedy of human enterprise.

Brandon hints that this world's superheroes develop appetites for tragedy. "There is the tragedy of a man who works very hard and never gets what he wants," says Kissinger. "And there is the even more bitter tragedy of a man who fully gets what he wants and finds out that he doesn't want it."

When Kissinger was the age of the little boy on Fifty-seventh Street, he was thrown out of his school, his father was fired, his humiliated family got out of Nazi Germany and made their way to America. Thirty years later, risen out of humiliation, he merged with that other survivor of insult and injury, the nervous brooder Richard Nixon.

Two awkward-looking, magnetic, tenacious, finicky, corny, witty, suspicious, loyal, cold, tender men, our Lears, our Oedipuses. Even as they demythologized the world of foreign policy, the vocabulary of tragedy sneaked into their speech: honor and humiliation, agony and transcendence.

The worried little black face was my tunnel into the Kissinger-Nixon world. It turned out that their grand design, "the retreat of American power," the mutual acknowledgment of weakness by the superpowers, rested, in a sense, on that little boy: "The rebellions in the American ghettos and among the workers of Poland were signals no government could ignore."

Some day, anyway, the Great Designers, whose tragedies are composed of the bones of their subjects, may yield to those who will not be allowed to pay that price for their great designs; they will be supplanted by men who concentrate on doing what they can to see that the sadness in a boy's face comes from some ordinary small thing like a fight with a sister or a missed assignment.

Home Truths

Hit 'em where they ain't.

WILLIE KEELER

The pentagon is flat and called a plate.
Or home. You start there and try hard to return.
You can walk, hit or get hit. Don't strike air,
or hit too close to *them*. Time doesn't matter.
Matters take their own time in this green space.
(Night can be as luminous as day.)

They are spread out in this space. Nine of them:
fly-catchers, ground-coverers, ball-stoppers,
there to see your nullity's preserved.
You'll recognize them; their color's different,
and you're at the eye-end of their funnel.
Despite the set-up, remember it's a game.

As long as you get back where you began,
you're somehow more than what you started as.

Nixon on Nixon

Delightful was a codeword we used to connote trouble. We did not have a codeword for disaster.

from the diary of Tricia Nixon Cox

*A*UGUST 6, 1974. The Presidency is falling around his ears, there are no forces left to rally. Even George Wallace won't help; he doesn't hear too well on the phone, besides he doesn't think it's his place to persuade Representative Flowers to vote against impeachment. The family listens to the "smoking gun" tape, is somewhat shaken but rallies round. Julie rushes over to the White House and leaves a passionate note of support on Daddy's pillow: don't decide for a week, I love you.

Passionate, yes, sincere, yes, but also, yes, dated (August 6), for, after all, even in passionate haste, a Nixon cannot forget that every scrap of paper is historic.

History, in full regalia, bedevils our recent presidents. The shallower the historical imagination, the more historical trinkets are assembled. Johnson had squads of photographers recording every presidential belch. And Nixon, that lover of privacy, installed the recording machines. No reader of the *Memoirs* will imagine this President destroying those tapes.* Wipe out the footprints on the sands of time that lives of great men leave behind them? (Grandma Milhouse had written the Longfellow lines under Richard's thirteenth birthday present, a picture of Lincoln. It is never

---

* *The Memoirs of Richard Nixon* (New York: Grosset and Dunlap, 1978).

too early to instill historic ambition.) Even when some footprints lead to smoking guns, History will exonerate the well-meaning. This book charts the good intentions of its author.

> if any here,
> By false intelligence, or wrong surmise,
> Hold me a foe;
> If I unwittingly, or in my rage,
> Have aught committed that is hardly borne
> By any in this presence, I desire
> To reconcile me to his friendly peace.

This is not the King Richard for whom our Richard was named—that was Richard Lion-Heart, Richard "Yea and Nay"—but Shakespeare's hypocritical charmer, Richard Crouchback. The lines do describe one function of these memoirs; but only one. This book is composed, not merely assembled, and I think the composition is meant to reflect a deeper kind of tragedy than that of *Richard III*.

In the last days, Nixon's son-in-law, Edward Cox, warns him that resignation will not end his troubles, the legal jackals are getting ready to pick his bones.

> I said to him [Cox] that this was just like a Greek tragedy: you could not end it in the middle of the second act, or the crowd would throw chairs at the stage. In other words, the tragedy had to be seen through until the end as fate would have it.

The story has at least the ingredients of tragic narrative: idyllic beginnings among orange blossoms, mountains, ocean, a haunted house ("viewed with awe, approached with caution"); devoted, hard-working, God-worshipping parents (bad-tempered Dad,[†] saintly Mom); early hard work, music lessons, dreams of far places (his favorite magazine the *National Geographic*); early encounters with death and separation (mother off to nurse one of the two brothers who died); school triumphs (debating, acting, student politics) and disappointment (losing the class presidency, the dream of going to school in the East frustrated by the medical expenses of the dying brother); doing well at Whittier; becoming a Tolstoyan (intoxicated by his pacifism and spirituality); winning a scholarship to Duke Law School; doing well but failing—again in the East—to get a job in New York or with the FBI; joining the oldest law firm in Whittier; marrying the pretty teacher met at the tryout of the local drama club; then the war, the OPA and—despite Quaker and Tolstoyan pacifism—the Navy; the invitation to run for Congress and the long public career ending in the unique resignation in the face of impeachment. If not exactly a "mirror for magistrates," why isn't the story an historical tragedy?

Two reasons, I think. One is a profound confusion of historical glitter and reality, and the second, which accounts for the first, is the disproportion between experience and character. That first modern confessor, Rousseau, wrote that unless a man had certain key experiences, he would never discover his own nature. There is, I think, a corollary of this which applies not only to Nixon but to many public men whose experience is so various, complex, and intense. It is that the experience exceeds the capacity of the man to absorb it into his nature. Forced to appear as if he understands and cares deeply about everything, the man manufactures an air of concern which floats over a

---

[†] Nixon traces his "aversion to personal confrontations" to that temper.

spreading hollowness. The public characters of Johnson and Nixon testify to the strains of the condition. The Nixon Zigzag—in which he must show that his choice has always bypassed the easy, popular options—shows up not only in public decision (approving the Huston antiterrorist plan) but private ones (the difficult decision to keep his mother in a nursing home). We all have difficult decisions, few of us are strong enough to dismiss public opinion (à la Tawney's description of the Puritan "spiritual athlete" dismissing "concern with the social order as the prop of weaklings and the Capua of the soul"), but Nixon not only constantly thinks of the gallery but wants to make it think he is the solitary soul driving on no fuel but his principles and beliefs. This discrepancy partly accounts for the length of his book.

Length, though, contributes something important here. As it wears on, hundred pages after hundred pages, Nixon wearies of façade, and the book erodes into a kind of honesty (which also characterized the last—first-shown—David Frost interview). It's as if the "ordeal" (Nixon's word) of writing the book had peeled off the make-up. Virtue is often just exhausted vice. (The tormentor may surrender to his victim.) The length of this book then serves a historic, if not a literary purpose. Nixon shows more of himself than he probably intended to show. Indeed, this book makes the other presidential memoirs—Van Buren's, Grant's, Truman's, Eisenhower's, and LBJ's are the ones I know—seem prudish, if not devious.

It is in part the pressure of this Age of Openness. So much has already come out that anything less than what Mr. Honest-man (*Ehrlich-man*) called "a modified limited hang-out" would seem like fraud. It is also because Nixon has some skill with words. He does not have a profound

intellect or imagination, his observations are usually puerile—unless he is estimating the deceptiveness of enemies
(in negotiations or poker)—his style is unenchanting,
his humor febrile, but he is a trained debater, a lawyer, a
skilled interpreter and planter of verbal signals, and he belongs to a Quaker tradition of self-accountability. So this
book brings us diary entries which show him wrestling
with himself (not championship matches but matches nonetheless) as well as descriptions of meetings with Mao and
Brezhnev which have intrinsic historic interest. There is a
fine long account of the negotiations with the North Vietnamese in which Nixon's tenacity and boldness appear to
count for more than Kissinger's mastery of detail, persis-
tence, and subtlety. (Nixon's generous treatment of his pro-
fessorial *Wunderkind* is one of many generous tributes in a
book which also features the "other Nixon," vengeful, suspicious, and mean-spirited, never failing to kick his enemy's other cheek).

Indeed the book has a great deal for every Nixonian
(haters and sympathizers, students and decoders). Read
closely, it reveals much. There are many themes more or
less dropped into the pile: the penduluming between East
and West; the contempt for the American establishment
and the awe of exotic gurus (Adenauer, Rhee, Whittaker
Chambers); the desire to love one's enemies (see the refer-
ences to John Dean). An essay could be written about the
role of food: from the Nixon family market and mother's
angel-food cake to the final day in the White House when
he treats himself at last to an orgy of corned beef and
poached eggs (instead of the loathed wheat germ). Food
stands for pleasure self-denied. His first inkling that he
might be president came at a Republican dinner when Tom
Dewey told him it was in the cards if he didn't get fat. The

book's rare lyricism pours over food, over Connally's country sausage and Ike's homemade watermelon preserves—although this has more to do with Ike's grudging acceptance of him than sensual pleasure. That the Pentagon codewords for another secret indulgence, the bombing of Cambodia, were operations Menu, Breakfast, and Lunch, will make the essay black comedy.

There is a secret affair with something more important than food: tourism. Would he ever have eaten Peking duck with Chou En-lai if it hadn't been for his desire to have the world rapidly delivered in pretty packages? Thank God for the *National Geographic* and for Hollywood's old soundstage glamorizing of exotic places.

Foreign Policy. Nixon's *specialité*. To debate—through moderators, no confrontations—to confer at summits, this is the Nixonian passion. And to ground this passion in concepts of world order as spelled out by an exotically accented professor, a philosophic authenticator of cultural depth, this is the life.

Back home though, the slovenly, selfish, disorderly politicians spewed up by those professional distorters, The Media, threaten to pick up the pieces of his triumph. He has to guard his flanks; the key is information, and he uses the same instruments of government his predecessors got away with using to get it.

Fatal convergence of foreign negotiation and domestic fly-swatting: and Nixon's presidency comes apart. The book ends with a "scene" "like a frame of film forever frozen": not the haunted house near Yorba Linda, but that other haunted house, "viewed with awe and approached with caution," before which the crowd stands: the "elegant curve of the South Portico: balcony above balcony" and "someone waving a white handkerchief from the window of the Lincoln Bedroom." A "final salute" and into the helicopter, Pat saying "It's so sad. It's so sad," and it's off for Andrews "where *Air Force One* was waiting for the flight home to California."

Is *The Memoirs of Richard Nixon* a good book?

Does the earth have a good moon?

It's the only one we have. And, as one of Nixon's diary entries puts it, "you can see in the moon whatever you want to see."

Kissinger on Kissinger

Señor mío, it would be a good thing if we were to go a little
farther, for I am sure we should be able to find someplace
where we might quench this terrible thirst that is consuming us.

CERVANTES, *Don Quixote*

OCTOBER 8, 1972. A cool October Sunday in a country
house which the painter Léger bequeathed to the Communist Party. In a "large quiet room, hung with abstract paintings," Henry Kissinger experiences the greatest moment of his career. The "droning voice" of the "elderly revolutionary" Le Duc Tho delivers the peace terms for which Kissinger has worked so long. That night he walks the Paris streets, surrounded by the history which "inspires but . . . does not overwhelm." Half a week later, he flies home "in blissful ignorance of the future," that Watergated future which will nullify the meaning of his deepest moment.

Over and over again, this enormous book* tolls the catastrophic bell. In Peking, the tottering "colossus," Chairman Mao, tells Nixon no, his writings have not changed a world, only "a few places in Peking." Every public accomplishment is sabotaged by foolishness or chance, by "the limits of human foresight" or by "the wickedness of objects" (which "always" rolls coins under beds and bureaus). The book's last page sees its second-greatest figure, the courageous, absurd, victorious hermit, Richard Nixon, "on a pinnacle, that was soon to turn into a precipice."

After another diplomatic triumph, a lyric Kissinger re-

---

*Henry Kissinger, *The White House Years* (Boston: Little, Brown, 1979).

turns to the Kremlin "while the first rays of sunlight" fall "on its golden domes, ochre walls, and red brick battlements." He is "seized by one of those rare moments of hope that makes the endless struggle with the contingent endurable for statesmen." The gloomy, bold, Byzantine Nixon is the incarnation of that struggle, the icon of a human perversity which despises its own triumph even more than it does those who thwart it.

A book is like a crisis. While chronicling commotion, its author works in an intense, exhilarating, and exhausting solitude to strip the essential from the inessential. When a serious and gifted man like Henry Kissinger labors on a book, it becomes—even more than a crisis he's resolved— the signature which will survive him. Such a book may be intended only as "an historical record" (Kissinger's words), but the manner in which it heaves itself into literary orbit against the mass and gravity of its fact reveals and then recreates its author.

This book is—to use the blurb word which is a favorite of its author—monumental, and like many such solid commemorations, its form is not beautiful. It is repetitive, needlessly detailed, and sometimes clumsily ornamented. More effort has gone into assembling than composing it. Nonetheless, it is much closer to being a great memoir than just the memoir of a great man. Its author has opened himself up. In this Age of Openness, he finds a thousand ways of bursting through reticence and policy. The work is lanced with portraiture, with lyric jets, with thumbnail essays on bureaucracy, national styles, crisis management, the rhythms of diplomacy. And it is lit by that comic spirit which far more than hope converts the *endless struggle* (Hegel) into a great life game. (A game that now and then is a death game. See the scene in which Nixon, infuriated by his own—wise—restraint towards North Korea, eases himself by ordering extra bombing raids. On Vietnam!) The comedy of Kissinger is seldom lethal, and it is as indispensable to the health of his book as it was to the author.

There is a great variety of comedy in this literary tundra: scenes, such as the one in which Nixon and Brezhnev, lost in the technicalities of weaponry, begin arguing for each other's positions; farcical portraits like those of the charming political cutthroat, Melvin Laird, the brilliant fantasist general, Vernon Walters, and that decent barbarian dullard, H. R. Haldeman, whose cretinous myrmidons of publicity work out the traffic jams in Rome and Belgrade which enable their image-mad President to take advantage of "photo opportunities." Above all, there are the two seriocomic portraits which dominate the unmonumental portions of the book.

Most literary portraits fall into already-created types. So, in *White House Years*, we have another version of Don Quixote and Sancho Panza: the foolish, courageous, intuitive, confused, half-mad, self-made presidential knight and the paunchy, shrewd factotum who both sees through and helps create his master's dream. It will be a surprise to many that the Henry Kissinger who lives in this book is not a profound thinker, not the "great man" of history. He is, he knows, too healthy-minded, too worldly to be one of those "obsessive monomaniacs" (to use two of the words which, with *Byzantine, geopolitical, folklore, unsentimental,* and *nuance* compose the book's ground base) who become the world's presidents, premiers, revolutionaries, and colossi. Kissinger understands the great thirst of these men, and, like Sancho, helps his master "in an age of Iron, try to revive what is known as the Golden Age." But though he rages, weeps, and laughs en route, it is the laughter of the

ground bass?

thinker which dominates. And it is comedy, not tragedy, of which his literary style is capable.

Has our Sancho written a great book?

No, for it is the world's Cervanteses who do that. He has, however, written a splendid one, formed—and de-formed—by manifold obligations, but redeemed by an honesty and intelligence which reveal even more than he may have intended.[†]

[†]A somewhat harsher view of the book, its edematous self-justification and "sog-gy, proustian tea-bags" is in "Missingeria," *Georgia Review*, Spring 1980. The comedy of the book might have looked more like hangman's humor a few years earlier. (I was writing pieces comparing the Nixon world to the Oprichniki spies and terrorists of Ivan the Terrible.)

Off the Sleeve

March 17, 1977

The Boss is away. Stroking the citizens of Clinton, Massachusetts and the world, the last at the United Nations, where he sends out the good old—but apparently disturbing—word that the United States doesn't like to see people shoved into loony bins for saying that things can be improved in Prague, Moscow, Guatemala City or Washington, D.C.

In Washington, a perfection of spring. The cherry trees are little Japanese gentlemen blooming in the wisdom not of Tanizaki's mad old lustful man, but the pictures of Hokusai and even more venerable depictors. The flowers peek and smile: "More of us are on the way." I walk around the Washington I haven't seen in eleven years; and it comes back, the formidable marble miles, the intermissions of sunken plazas, the magnolias, the squares, the odd thumbs of nineteenth- and—rare and getting rarer—eighteenth-century nooks. Planes almost slice the forehead off the Lincoln Memorial. My pal, a resident reporter, says congressmen won't take the trouble to go out to Dulles, won't rearrange the flight plans. It's as if Washington permitted an hourly staging of *Black Sunday* (a film about a dirigible crashing into the Orange Bowl).

I call Walter Wurfel, the president's deputy press secretary. "He's with the president in New York," says an amiable southern voice, masculine, youthful. The phone's rung ten times before being picked up.

"May I leave a message?"

"I'll go find a secretary."

A wait. The search is useless, the voice, laughing, is back on the phone. "Doesn't seem to be anyone around."

Am I calling City Hall in Duffville some Saturday afternoon in the deer season? No, it's the White House at three o'clock on a March Thursday.

"May I leave a message with you?"

"Surely."

I leave the reminder that I'm the fellow from Chicago Wurfel asked to come down and talk about a "down-to-earth"—his description, not mine—piece on the president. I was thinking of John Hersey's piece on Truman. Or Ford. (Small pickings there.) "I'll call again tomorrow."

When I get back from my walking tour and supper, there's a message taped to the stairs (the routine in the amiable house in which I'm staying). "Tom Drummond returned your call from the White House."

I call Tom Drummond; he's just responding to my call. (Of such is the kingdom of electronic nullity.) Next day, I do get Wurfel on the phone, and we set up an appointment on Monday morning so I can get "cleared" over the weekend. (I give him birthdate and social security number. "That's all I need.")

The weekend is mine. I have a few friends, a few names. I call them. Most are out of town. But enough are there, and I'm suddenly energized by the ease of my effort. Since I don't give a damn whether or not I do a piece about Carter, my head does some work for me and thinks out a project which does excite me. Till then, the idea was simply an energy overflow from the completion of a four-year-long book. Now it takes shape. I'll spend three days a year watching Carter and see what happens to him over the presidential term. I'll have both the propinquity and the scarcity which gives distance. I won't be writing retrospectively like aides, friends, assistants, ministers of state, I won't be writing postparturition memoirs. I'll be testing Lord Acton's famous maxim in terms of sharp impressions. Monet with a pen.

In the bathtub I conjure up my Monday conversation with Wurfel, then advance it to Jody Powell, then—getting a little weary of it—to Hamilton Jordan, and finally Carter. The president—I call him Mr. Carter or Jimmy—and I get on splendidly.

He's for real, he's smart, we hit it off. I've only asked for five minutes of his time, I finally have to haul myself off after an hour. He tries to pull me back, but I remember the nation and tell him to get back to work. His respect grows. End of bath.

Jim Rowe, the gray eminence of several Democratic presidencies, returns a call. It's really he I should talk to, a vessel of hardly decanted inside dope. I know his daughter a bit, a dear girl to whom I once suggested doing a book about her father. When I tell him this, he seems puzzled, relieved nothing came of it; yet he seems ready to talk. How long will I be around? Not long enough. All right, drop him a note next time, he'll "set aside some time" for me.

I bus down Mausoleum Alley, wander the terrible corridors of the Senate Office Building, notice George McGovern's plaque. I'd spent a long Chicago day with him back in 1970, a fine fellow, already en route to his catastrophe. He has a few minutes before his lunch date. We talk in his new, large office. I remark its handsomeness. He colors, is apologetic, he thinks he'll convert some of it into work space. The deep eyes, oddly set as if they belong to a different, more statuesque head, seem to me touched with aborted purpose. He seems shrunken in his dark suit. (Overreading?) How is he on Carter? He is not "exuberant." "The man's a genius of public relations. That's about it." Rat that I am, I ask what he would have done in his first days in office. He swallows, the forehead glows, but he says quietly the war dominated everything then, he'd planned to announce a way to end it—an echo falls off the words— then declare a general amnesty. The rest would follow. We talk of his recent visit with Castro and his piece in the Sunday *Times Magazine.* He has not heard from the White House. "I didn't expect to hear from them." He'd turned in a report, perhaps that was of some use. He praises the beauty of the Capitol. "Such a beautiful building for a democracy."

"If you like Michelangelo and the Pantheon," say I. (Later that afternoon, a fellow I haven't seen in thirty years gives me a speech he just gave on art and democracy in which he twits the classical marmoreality of the Capitol. Is this what is meant by *Zeitgeist?*) Still, for more than South Dakota, the Capitol continues the dream of grandeur, the organization of Rome, the genius of Brunelleschi and Michelangelo. Why have a Saarinen arch or a Wright seashell as our legislative factory?

I pass Humphrey's office, go in and manage to draw out a curious press secretary. Since I wear a vest, I get much respect. But the Senator's off to Minneapolis. Can I come back? Can he call me? No, I just wanted to talk with him. No importance. The word in town is that the poor fellow's dying, that his famous, frantic energy is coiled into gallows humor. Still, he's in there pitching, and the cast of characters in his office is interesting, a rabbinical-looking delivery man and a large-bellied black man in gold sport shirt and mauve slacks. (Are they living decor, always on tap?)

I look in on a hearing. Three senators, including the neat little Mustache Pete, Hayakawa, listen to heavy-voiced testimony about—I think—the common situs bill. Hayakawa asks about comparative absentee figures in the construction and other industries, is reminded by Chairman Hatch that the area was ruled out of bounds. I'd like to talk to Hayakawa but can't wait out another half hour of testimony in a room as smoky as this one.

The rest of the weekend I see friends, museums, kites flying in the Mall, the enormous hall in the National Portrait Gallery where Walt Whitman nursed soldiers in the Civil War. Outside the Corcoran Gallery, laid out like living sculpture near the air vents, is a cluster of bums. They are a breath's distance from the White House. Is this India? New Delhi? (Another imperial superstructure risen from slum and bustee, London *redivivus*; that is, Athens *redivivus* in its *n*th life.) The human emblem of great social failure.

Monday, the White House. My hostess braves the traffic (there are no cabs afloat) and gets me to within a couple of blocks of the northwest gate. I'm in a little anteroom surrounded by—mostly Japanese—photographers.

Bless my vest. The security cop spots me, I banker my way through the photographic canaille, give my name, get a visitor's badge and walk the curving driveway, enter the press lobby, go down a hall lined with puerile etchings ("A Fireman's Life" and the "Cares of a Family," the family being avian) to a small room where three secretarial desks crowd each other. There isn't much action, only joshing, phone-ringing, a few people coming in and out. Under

glass, like plucked, stuffed, baked game birds, are ticker-
tape machines. The UP keys type out earthquake predic-
tion techniques in China: "Snakes came out of hibernation,
small pigs bit each other, cows fought, deer ran away, tur-
tles jumped out of the water and cried, hens flew to tree-
tops, geese panicked." It sounds like an Auden poem.

The AP ticker reports the impending White House reception of Premier Fukuda of Japan. Ah so. That explains
the photographers' complexion.

I wait half an hour, someone in Jody Powell's office sees
me looking at his feet on his grand desk and shuts his door.
Then I see Wurfel, who is pleasant, bright, soft-mustached,
blue-eyed and surprised at my project. "You mean you
wouldn't publish till after the election? You know we work
on a half-hour deadline around here." He asks if what I'm
planning is psychohistory. "No way." Wurfel works up
kindly enthusiasm. "This could be as important for the
presidency as for Carter." What a note. He must have been
taping the bathtub. In the manner of my reverie, he seems
more reluctant than I to end the talk.

His secretary must be tuned to our good feeling. She
takes my arm, offers me a little Japanese flag, and we go
out to the lawn to help receive Premier Fukuda. I go with
the reporters and stand across from Vance, Mondale, Mrs.
Vance, an admiral in many spangles (who turns out to be
Turner of the CIA, getting a last fling in his braid). Vance's
hands slice and circle, he's illustrating points for two Japanese gentlemen and Mondale (the Japanese are identified
for me by my neighbor: they're the ambassador and foreign secretary). Mondale has a sweet-bird-of-youth face
that I think will never adorn a quarter. But, who knows—
men become their offices.

The Vance crowd stick near their name plates. (This is how it's done.) A voice spooks out of the glittering house: "The president of the U-nited States and Mrs. Carter." Hand in hand come the little couple, mouthing happy talk with each other. They smile at their government, at the Vances, Turners, Mondale. Who now are all attention. Apparently sight of the Boss does something to the spine. We all wait, the little couple on the driveway and the entourage. A limousine sweeps around the bushes. Out steps a smiling old cherry tree of a man and a terrific little dish, something out of illustrations of Sei Shonagun's *Pillow Book*. I'm surrounded by clicks and buzzes. "Who's the chick?" "Not his wife?" "Daughter?" "Interpreter?" "His lunch?"

Diplomatic arms are circling, Carter's and Fukuda's, Rosalynn's and the dish's. The men climb the reviewing stand, the band plays anthems, cannons boom (orange flowers puff in the gray smoke), flags bend, the great white obelisk looks goofily down on all of us, and, half a mile away, the cherry blossoms wave from the Tidal Basin. A beautiful scene.

The troops are reviewed. Carter walks oddly, leg caving slightly at the knee, the walk of a marionette whose puppet master is slightly looped. Back at the stand, a gracious speech. "We've arranged this weather for the prime minister," and something about our two powerful nations, the cherry trees preparing to blossom forth. (Premier Fukuda, who's actually noticed them, says later, "How nice to see the blossoms in bloom.") Fukuda speaks. Carter appears to be tuned to hidden music. (Is he plugged into his office hi-fi?) Mrs. Carter is looking, no, glaring at me. Am I staring too hard at everything? Do I bulk too grossly over my Japanese neighbors? Do I have—despite my banker's worsted—an assassin's look? I stare back, her eyes shift. In my heart, there is a small whiff of lust.

Vance too has given me a quizzical look. Has he seen my assessment of him and his wife? For I overplay my impressions (what else do I have?) and see a certain bleakness in their kindly, dutiful stiffness. There have been too many scheduled events in those lives.

The speech is over. I ask my Japanese neighbor if the premier speaks elegant Japanese.

"He not talk from text. He speak off the sleeve."

The premier beams, waves. The Vance crowd applauds. I wave and exchange understanding looks with the old blossomer. He, his dish, and the Carters walk up the beautiful curved staircase and stand momentarily, regally on the Truman balcony before going inside. The Vance crowd follows.

Carolyn, the secretary, has my arm. "I thought I'd lost you." We walk back with Ann Compton, a hefty young woman from ABC who says she asked Carter in church yesterday morning what he was doing about the spring. "He said, '*Es muy frio.*'" (This remark is now part of the sacred text.)

There is a briefing. An angry Japanese summons his crew, taps them rapidly on the shoulder and, at the last minute, halts his fingers inches from my blue worsted. A pretty blonde complains about all the cherry-blossom talk. "Oy vey," she says, in a pronunciation not learned at mother's breast. "Where are we gonna get substance?" She moves towards the briefing room, I follow but am told, "It's only for Pool."

I've had it. I walk down the driveway, surrender my pass, and enter the banal world. A well-dressed woman hands me a mimeograph sheet about her son, a Vietnam flier who was captured. "In not demanding his release, President Carter is guilty of violating Nick Brook's human rights."

A week later, back in Chicago, my pal John Hope Franklin hails me on Fifty-eighth Street. I tell him my White House project, does he know any comparable pieces I should read. He'll let me know, and meanwhile tells me *his* White House anecdote. He's part of a committee to recommend ambassadors. They were in the Oval Office the other day, Harriman, Rusk, and the like. Carter came in, they all stood and Carter said, "You mustn't do that." He blew a kiss to a blonde woman. "She was for me even before I was myself." He'd talked for half an hour about their job, the sort of appointments he wanted to make, said he wanted to see each of them individually, he hoped they'd excuse him today. As he left, they stood up again. "I said you mustn't do that."

The Office. The Office. Or Washington, Washington.

Another pal of mine's just been feted there.* Bill Moyers introduced him with such defamatory charm he felt he couldn't hold his head up. "All these senators and Supreme Court justices will think I'm a fink." As for Washington? "Glorious, foolish, excited, wicked, tricky. The whole bit."

As to my Carter piece. "He doesn't want your kind of coverage."

Nonetheless, I write up my proposal, studded with gems from Plutarch, Thucydides, the memoirs of Grant, Van Buren, Ike. The King Tut show is wowing Washington, Carter has had a private glimpse, has come out officially impressed.

---

* Saul Bellow.

"I want to do something on Carter that'll last a bit, like the gold head of Tut." I don't stint on self-praise, and enclose a couple of my books.

Perhaps they do me in. In any case, five weeks go by and there's no peep from Wurfel. Can they possibly have more important things to do? I wait. The night Carter makes his "moral equivalent of war" talk I call him—Wurfel—at home to tell him the speech knocked me out. "It sounded like the man himself."

"He worked on all three drafts of it."

"Anything doing on the historic portrait line?"

"It's under active consideration. No gobbledygook."

This little clinker from the 1940s—my growing time, not Wurfel's—reassures me. "I trust you completely."

May comes and goes, and lovely is the rose, but no word from the West Wing. By June, I'm into another piece, but little wheels are still spinning around the imagined Oval Office. I write Powell, not Wurfel, and ask if my project is up the flue. "I wouldn't want me around if I were Carter," I throw in as defensive vaccine. But I also supply an alternative. "Give me an hour with him to talk about *The Leopard*." (I hear that he's reading this wonderful piece of Sicilian Faulkneriana.) "And that kind of thing." I add that for form, and, as form goes, I actually draw a response, not from Powell but from his epistolary alter ego, Wurfel. "I have a stack of your letters. You've earned an answer." The answer, he says he's sorry to say, is negative. Nor have they approved any other "book project." (The marginal courtesies of consolation.)

I've been learning modern Greek in preparation for a Schliemannian tour of Mycenae, Knossos, Phaestos. I don't learn easily, I don't learn well, but after twenty sessions with the ear phones in the language lab, I can work out some poems of Elytis and Cavafy (at least while Edmund Keeley's translations are across the page). It's from one of these, a Cavafy sonnet called "*Krymena*" ("Hidden Things") that I draw my invisible portrait of the Stern-protected president.

From everything I did and said
no one can find out who I was.
An obstacle there altered
the ways and manner of my life . . .
Only from my most obscure actions
and least noted writing
will I be understood.
Perhaps, though, it doesn't really matter,
this discovery of me. . . .

The following five little pieces are literary steam blown after reading the newspaper or watching the news. Only the most benign—the one on the Post Office—was published (and that on the Op Ed page of the New York Times*).*

Carter into Liddy

IN 1800 the poet Wordsworth described the causes of what he felt was the deterioration of the national mind: "The most effective of these causes are the great national events which are daily taking place, and the increasing accumulation of men in cities, where the uniformity of their occupations produces a craving for extraordinary incident, which the rapid communication of intelligence hourly gratifies."

April 25, 1980 saw the broadcast of that extraordinary incident, the aborted rescue of the Teheran hostages. The words and faces of broadcasters were full of the special tension produced by the pleasure of communicating a peril not directly one's own.

The same news programs showed the different face of Barbara Timm, the mother of one of the young hostages. Her words flowed directly from the need to protect her son: she urged a policy of mutual understanding based on continued talks. She was followed by Henry Kissinger, grave with his heavy burden, the waging of the great geopolitical struggle to which everything else is subordinate. He approved the mission, was of course unhappy at its failure, but felt that the activity itself was a sign to the world that the United States would not remain forever passive. (This listener felt that a source of such revolutions as the Iranian one might be a despair that the Kissingers of the United States and the Soviet Union consumed too much of the world's goods in their monstrous competition.)

As for President Carter, a subset of the Acton Law ("Power tends to corrupt . . .") seemed to be at work, the Lex Liddyensis: "When in doubt, clout." (Or: In quadrennial Novembers, every baffled President tends to become G.-Gordon-Liddyfied.) A low-key, intelligent man who spent two campaign and two-plus presidential years deploring the mentality of crisis, the President was now a victim of it. (Soviet and Iranian terrorists had helped, yes, but it was more a Liddyan craving for the extraordinary and a desire to gratify it in the electorate which accounted for it.) How some of us wish it were Lex Timm instead of Lex Liddy at work. If Amy Carter were in that embassy, would the President have dispatched the helicopters?

The United States has a poor record of rescue missions: Bay of Pigs, Mayaguez, Con Tay. Entebbe dazzles us, but Entebbe was a Timm-like, not a Liddy-like mission. It stemmed from much greater national desperation. (If Israelis could be kidnapped in the neutral air, no Israeli was safe.) Americans are too powerful to have to show their muscles. Yet those whose job is to supply hourly gratifications of excitement pick up those specialists in disaster (unemployed statesmen and campaigning legislators) to transform the world's ordinary grit into jewels of crisis. The worst consequence of this effort may be the deterioration of the national mind which Wordsworth worried about in far less agitated times.

Radix Malorum Est Cupiditas

A SICK ANIMAL flails unseen tormentors. So we lash the *causes* of inflation: OPEC, monetary policy, federal spending, presidential ineptitude, the winter. Most of us, though, smell the real trouble spot, know it's the same old place. Inside Me. Inside You.

Greed, vanity, selfishness, exhibitionism, the old sermon topics, they're all here euphemized as "the profit motive" and institutionalized in management training programs, corporate progess. "Some lousy second quarter you got here, Gridley."

Here's a little scene from the Age of Inflation: Time, the bicentennial summer; Place, the home grounds of the presidential candidate. Hungry reporters buy lemonade and peanut-butter sandwiches made and sold by the candidate's little daughter. The candidate observes, then calls across, "Charge 'em double." Daughter, a one-person Organization of Peanut-Butter-Sandwich Producers, hearkens to the instruction, doubles the price, and is on the great inflationary road to success.

The candidate himself has done very well in peanut butter, but for years, he has been in another sort of enterprise, politics, and one hears that something important has happened to him after a political defeat. He's suffered depression (a word which doubles for financial and personal trouble) and taken to solitary walks and talks with a ministering sister. Another part of his nature has been nurtured to deal with the pain risen from the checked assertiveness. It's said that on a sort of preaching mission in the North, he's experienced what amounts to a ratification of his revamped will, though that has not deflected his ambition, only strengthened it for the terrible effort of his amazing campaign.

Now the ex-candidate proposes "voluntary guidelines" to control the great disease. Does he sense the root of individual *voluntas* in the fatigued phrase? Keyed to the duplex setup of his own will, does he believe that the *radix malorum* is indeed individual, not institutional, cupidity? (Chaucer's greedy Pardoner used *radix malorum* as his text. Knowing himself, he knew his customers.)

Let's render the text as "Greed's the root, Inflation the fruit." It's the greed which has less to do with appetite than punishment, more with hatred than love. Euphemisms pluck the string but introspection shows that the antique sin's alive and kicking.

And kicking the prosperous all over the world, in Teheran and Riyadh as well as New York and Topeka. Perhaps in these days, when China wants to set out on the long road, we might remind her and ourselves of one of her great texts (from the *Ta Hsio* or *Great Digest*): "The men of old wanting to spread the light which comes from looking into the heart and then acting, first set up good government. . . . Wanting good government in their states . . . they rectified their own hearts."

Bicentenary Musing

IN THE VARIETY and range of our pleasures, the great majority of Americans unite every refinement of convenience, elegance, and splendor, whatever soothes our vanity and gratifies our sensuality.

I write—or at least adapt—this sentence from Gibbon's description of the Rome of the Antonines while millions of Americans live on the dole, millions more work at jobs which drug their sensibility, urban children go to school with bellies locked in constipation for fear of being brutalized by their peers in lavatories, and while the country's political leaders mouth rhetoric whose diction and rhythm alone would murder the significance stranded in it, a significance usually so befouled with rusted policy its inadequacy is plain even to them and leads them into private—but well-leaked—jeremiads.

Nonetheless, the Gibbonian description holds. The commercial network brings to most Americans incredible varieties of goods and services which are consumed with regal disregard for the difficulties which produce and distribute them. And wherever the electronic gospel reaches, the American dream of luxurious transportation, entertainment, habitation, and the means of self-expression flourishes.

America itself is rocked by the Law of Self-Contradictory Pleasure: foods, toys, automobiles, television sets, highrises, medicines, and birth-control devices seethe with chemical, structural, or distributive menace. Not that many are ready to throw in the great towel. Mechanisms of special interest defend even the flimsiest and most perilous of our goods, and these are underwritten by a frenzied contentment with the system which so easily confuses liberty and air conditioning, pluralism and the supermarket.

While our two-hundredth anniversary is pumped into celebration by fiat and committee, we can notice the less-observed but most telling products of our luck, skill, and traditions. The "media" have made the average American as aware of his leaders' warts as Athenians were of their leaders' opinions. This has helped create a citizenry eager to both express and combat thousands of special interests. This massive individuation, along with the publication of the intimate, and the orchestration of "the peculiar," allows Americans to see themselves with a specialness that even a century ago was reserved only for poets, kings, and sages. A human with a car is a king on horseback; with a camera, a kind of Raphael or Fellini; with a tape recorder or transistor, a cut-rate Beethoven. Questioned in surveys, represented in polls, heard by telephone on the radio, featureable in a ubiquitous Candid Camera, the modern American is Someone to be Observed and Heeded; a Special Power.

Yet the great apparatus turns on itself. Millions yearn for more active employment of novel sensibilities and vitaminized limbs. There is the guided pursuit of erotic, culinary, and stylistic intricacy. People stake out plots of self-sufficiency accompanied by instructions in carpentry, plumbing, gardening. And resistance swells to the machinery which creates the means of such indulgence.

The resistance also underlies a narcotic culture whose easement has usually characterized resigned or floating worlds. Twelve-year-old Americans cluster around water-pipes like Indochinese ancients. The learned remark alterations in national mentality, the emphasis on the cerebral hemisphere which specializes in simultaneous integration rather than the one which controls sequential analysis. Arts and entertainments proffer the sensational burst instead of the consequential climax, the unexpected, the mystic, the absurd instead of the intricate and rational. Since sensation is brief, the dominant principle is Turnover.

Against this torrent is that enormous conservatism which is life itself, genetic compulsion, systemic repetition, body limitation; these need the fuel but cannot endure the vertigo of unremitting alteration.

The hunger for novelty and the antipathy to analysis endangers a system which is more and more dependent on expertise. The fragility of the great structure, its almost pathetic interdependence, does not consort well with the pace, shape, and color of American life which forms within the Storm of Self. Perhaps a bicentennial self will digest data instead of impressions and can express its individuality in expertise. (Already our grandeur lies more in the range and power of our learning and artistry than in pyramids.)

International commerce has been the chief mechanism of the American way of ease; it is said to have outstripped the political machinery which contained—if it didn't control —the older, local manufacture. This machinery existed largely for the equilibrium of factions and for national defense. More and more, though, it was the means of blowing national steam in xenophobic warfare.

Where will the boiling human energy go in the next century? Surely it will exert enormous pressure on every belief, instrument, and organization. Pacifying drugs, bread and circuses, may mute or deflect the pressure, but only the subtlest and most fluent leadership will be able to discover constructive outlets for it. The formation of planetary allegiance, the invention of significant occupations, the creation of an active peace which rests on neither vicious competition nor claustrophobic cooperation, these are endeavors fit to be the wish over the great American birthday cake.

In Defense of the Post Office

"**D**O YOU WANT the trains, airlines, utilities run like the Post Office?" For free-enterprisers, the Postal Service is the scapegoat, the butt, the despised and comic victim.

Where did we get the idea that the Post Office has to pay for itself? Or to be more self-sufficient than any other department of the government? Does the Interior Department have to fend for itself in an open market? Does the Defense Department have to support itself? Or Health, Education, and Welfare?

What is government about? The Interior Department watches over Indians and forests; HEW helps the helpless and rummages among educators and doctors; the Defense Department wards off threats (and offers a few). Splendid. We pay for these fine services and don't doubt for a minute that we should. From food stamps to the silvery stars on military shoulders, we pay and believe we are advancing the general welfare of the country.

But the Post Office. Ah, there's a grubby, slovenly enterprise, a classic pile of governmental misery. Anybody who wants to use its debased service had better be prepared to dig deep. Want to write Mom about Julie's graduation? O.K., pay for it. You pay for phone calls, don't you? If you had to fly to Mom, you'd pay plenty. So dig deep.

But wait, the government doesn't own the phones or planes. It does own the Post Office, and it has since the country started. Whoever thought that up must have had some notion it was a good thing. It must have something to do with general welfare.

In fact, what department of the government does more for the general welfare than the Post Office? And for less money? Go to thousands of towns at mail-delivery time, look at millions of faces opening up the small boxes that holds the day's mail. This is faring well. This is what we mean by human society. Transmission, articulation, the maintenance of networks of human feeling. In a nation that, like the universe itself, is in constant motion, mail not only keeps the parts in a kind of topological constancy, it builds a million histories. Every correspondent is the creator and the curator of the country's annals.

Not only the nation, but the world is brought together, and, with thin sheets of paper, preserved. Does this not advance health, education, welfare, national security? Letters are the externalized memory of society; and, in a way, are its essence.

All right, make the Post Office more efficient, but don't talk of penalizing those who write letters. If anything, talk of abolishing postage. Shouldn't the government—the collective we—encourage us to keep in touch, to spell out our thoughts and affections, spread intelligence, deepen fraternity, and memorialize our slivers of perception and insight? (Perhaps we should give redeemable stamps to correspondents).

In any case, the next time someone threatens to amputate postal service or otherwise menaces the creators and dispensers of private intelligence, grip him hard and suggest that HEW and the Defense Department be driven into the open market to peddle their distinguished services.

The Past and Future of Literature: A Play in Three Scenes

On December 3, 1979, the Supreme Court declined to hear the appeal of a novelist and a publisher who'd been successfully sued by a psychotherapist on the grounds that he'd been punitively maligned in a fictional portrait. The news resounded in literary space-time.

Scene i.

Time: 1300. Place: Somewhere in Italy. Persons: Dante and Publisher

DANTE: Then Vergil will hand me over to Beatrice.

PUBLISHER: Beatrice Portinari?

DANTE: That's the one.

PUBLISHER: We might ride with Vergil. No living descendants. But the Portinari's o-u-t. There's a husband, kids, and her uncle's a lawyer.

DANTE: All right. I'll call her Arabella.

PUBLISHER: Call her Giuseppe, she's still out. Let Vergil turn you over to a schnauzer. You're very good with animals.

DANTE: I've got lots of animals in parts one and two.

PUBLISHER: Didn't I tell you they're out? Every other line's about someone walking around the streets. Or someone with grandsons walking around. The Ulysses stuff is O.K. But call him Filippo. Cavalcanti's brother's named Ulisse.

DANTE: I don't know, Paolo. This poem's got a lot of dead weight. I'm not sure it's worth the trouble. I hear Can

Grande can use a Latin secretary. That might be the ticket for your old pal.

PUBLISHER: Why not? Lie low till the heat's off, then try a few sestinas.

Scene ii.

Time: 1600. Place: London. Persons: W. Shakespeare and Wise Friend

SHAKESPEARE: I see why the history plays have to go, but what's with Portia and Shylock?

WISE FRIEND: Not only do you have the Anti-Defamation League, you'll be hauled into court by Lopez. And the case'll be heard by Burleigh.

SHAKESPEARE: So?

WISE FRIEND: Burleigh's wife's called "the judge's judge." And what's your Portia? A fish peddler?

SHAKESPEARE: Wasn't much of a play anyway. But the Hamlet scheme's a good one.

WISE FRIEND: As idea, terrific. Just keep it to yourself.

SHAKESPEARE: The characters are Danes. Who can touch me in London?

WISE FRIEND: What a country kid you are, Willy. Did Lord Seale's widow marry his brother, or didn't she?

SHAKESPEARE: Claudius and Gertrude.

WISE FRIEND: You got it. You could make Claudius a friend of the family.

SHAKESPEARE: Not bad.

WISE FRIEND: And leave out that play within the play. The Seales love the theater.

SHAKESPEARE: Rosencrantz and his pal better go also. I'm sure the Seale kid went to college, may even have had a friend or two.

WISE FRIEND: Don't be such a wise guy. It doesn't become you. Polonius and the girl who goes off her rocker, that's also out.

SHAKESPEARE: Naturally, there must be twenty privy councilors with daughters in trouble. The thing to do is stick to sonnets.

WISE FRIEND: Only keep yours under your pillow. Every third nut in London's got a candidate for your *Schwarzerin*. One of them's bound to be right.

SHAKESPEARE: Little Annie bores the pants off me, but she's got a grand land operation going in Stratford. She could use someone with a head for figures.

WISE FRIEND: I'll sure miss you, sweet Willy.

Scene iii.

Time: 1990. Place: United States of America. Persons: Professor and Student of Contemporary Literature.

PROFESSOR: Done the assignment?

STUDENT: Sure, Prof.

PROFESSOR: O.K. What's the book about?

STUDENT: It begins with this thing, and then something pours in these three cups of—what do you call that white stuff?

PROFESSOR: Flour.

STUDENT: Riiight. Flour. See Flour's the main character.

CURTAIN

The Mandelstams

THE PLAGUE which spread over the Soviet Union was the extinction of personality; its cause, the rupture of old relationships. "We saw it come about in front of our very eyes," writes Nadia Mandelstam. "All intermediate social links, the family, one's circle of friends, class, society itself—each abruptly disappeared, leaving every one of us to stand alone before the mysterious force embodied in the State."

Thirty years earlier, the Flesh-eating Machine had devoured one of its greatest personalities, the poet Osip Mandelstam. For his widow, "there was no longer life or sense of life." If she was "saved," it was by "the thought of a 'you.' Instead of sense, my life had a concrete purpose: not to allow 'them' to stamp out all traces of the man I thought of as 'you,' to save his poetry."

In a way no Westerner I know can imagine, poetry—the unquantifiable registration of what is most original in personality—was the secret breath which sustained millions in their underwater Soviet existence. The great poets of the language had all been either killed, terrorized into suicide, or diminished into deformity or silence: Gumilev, Tsvetaeva, Babel, Yesenin, Mandelstam, Mayakovski, Blok, Akhmatova, Pasternak. Yet somehow, poetry broke through the stone of Soviet life. Decades after her work was officially obliterated, Akhmatova read in Moscow to cheering thousands. Stalin—the terrible essence of stone itself—inquired about the organization behind such a welcome.

Surviving.

"I survived only by a miracle or an oversight, which is

the same thing." Mrs. Mandelstam was a *stopiatnitsa*—a 'hundred-and-fiver, forbidden to live within 105 kilometers of large cities—she taught English linguistics, or, fired for sitting on a window sill instead of a chair and talking about Grimm's Law (of consonant change), lived off the charity of such friends as Akhmatova. The two women preserved in memory and talk the verse and personality of Mandelstam.

Every remarkable book writes itself (the author feels the true force, meaning and rhythm of the process en route) and many supply their own theory. Following—as always —her husband's notions, Nadia Mandelstam explains her unique books.* Tragedy doesn't exist on the Russian stage, but it lives in Russian narrative prose. As for prose, it is the "disjunctive expression" of life's continuum. So this book is as disjunctive as Montaigne's essays. Its tragic power is scattered in anecdotes, character studies, comic scenes, social observations, diatribes, textual and philosophical analysis. Mrs. Mandelstam is not the original Montaigne is; decades of survival life do not promote that idiomatic grace and inventiveness which mark what we call literary genius. Her book, though, is unique, and it offers the world another model of humanity, a brilliant, comprehensive devotion fixed by a tenacity of mourning which, oddly, is as much a source of joy as melancholy.

"In our age, everything has become so serious that any view not rooted in values sets the teeth on edge as a knife drawn over glass." The story of the Mandelstams is a great wad of gauze stuffed into the social world. It begins one May day in 1919 when the tiny, spirited, artistic twenty-

* *Hope against Hope* (New York: Atheneum, 1970) and *Hope Abandoned* (New York, Atheneum, 1974).

year-old Kiev girl meets the twenty-eight-year-old Petersburg poet. It is a month before Lenin has launched the first
terror (after the attempt on his life and the assassination of
Uritsky). The theory of terror has been readied. In *Gulag
Archipelago* I, Solzhenitsyn quotes a 1918 Lenin essay on
"the common, united purpose of a 'purge of the Russian
earth of all harmful insects.'" In September 1919 Lenin is
telling Gorki "not to spend his time whimpering over" that
species of insect he calls "rotten intellectuals."[†]

Yet it's still early, the golden time of revolution. The
Mandelstams have hope and even a small place in the new
world. Poets can serve, there is some traveling and a reporting job.[‡] Gorki himself allows Mandelstam a sweater,
though—disliking Mandelstam's poetry—Gorki crosses
out his request for trousers: "He'll manage without."

Mandelstam lacks that quantifying talent which makes
equations of pants and poems so easy for Gorki. He is the
real thing, one of fifty million who can express depth of
being in the same words the other forty-nine million plus use
to order hamburgers and court their sweethearts. In these
early days, such men sometimes had the protection of important officials. Bukharin was Mandelstam's "transmission belt," not only for special rations and trips to Ar-
menia, but for saving some of the insects the state purged
with such expertise.

In the thirties the system flowered into its perfect expression, the Georgian (or Ossetian) genius of human cynicism

---

[†] May 1981. I now think Solzhenitsyn's view of Lenin oversimplified to the point
of viciousness. It's partly the result of reading his lifeless *Lenin in Zurich*, partly
reading about a more human, if still grim Lenin in Justin Kaplan's biography of
Lincoln Steffens.
[‡] A brilliant 1923 interview with Ho Chi Minh (then known as Nguyen Ai Quoc)
isn't mentioned in Mrs. Mandelstam's book.

and meat-eating, Joseph Stalin. The collision between poet and dictator was as natural to human physics as the gravitational force between earth and a bit of dust. Every single personality of worth in the Soviet Union fell—one way or another—to that gross planet. The immediate cause of Mandelstam's fall doesn't matter; it was either his slapping Alexei Tolstoy (for being rude to Nadia) or writing a short poem about the Great Man:

> Words final as lead weights fall from his lips
> His cockroach whiskers leer
> His boottops gleam . . . And every killing is a treat
> For the broad-chested Ossete.

They carried Mandelstam off in 1934. But the "transmission belt" still functioned, and the Great Destroyer was informed about protests. A former divinity student, he understood the miracles of grace and remission. One night he made the famous telephone call to Pasternak which assured him that Mandelstam would be all right.

More or less. For four years, Osip and Nadia moved from place to place, "frightened by dogs barking," begging "alms from shadows." Then, nineteen years to the day after they'd met, it was over. Mandelstam was carried off into the oblivion of the death camps. Twenty years Nadia drifted over Russia in a semistupor. Then, during the Khrushchev "thaw," she got a room of her own and began writing her furious, funny, heartrending memorial of her life with Osip, its jokes, battles, tyrannies, and profundities. Its last page is a letter written in 1938:

> Osip, my beloved, faraway sweetheart, I have no words, my darling, to write this letter that you may never read. . . . I am

writing it into empty space. . . . I bless every day and every hour of our bitter life together, my sweetheart, my companion, my blind guide in life. . . . I speak only to you, only to you. You are with me always, and I who was such a wild and angry one and never learned to weep—now I weep and weep and weep. It's me, Nadia. Where are you? Farewell.

Getting at Oneself

He disposed of an immense quantity of solid food
with the benignity of a good soul who was feeding
someone else.

DICKENS,
Little Dorrit

The priests informed her [Helena, mother of Con-
stantine] that his cross had been thrown to the
ground and covered with excrements and filth. She
discovered the wood and built "the Church of the
Excrements" * over the place where those excrements had been.

IBN KHALDUN,
The Muqaddimah

*In fact, "Church of the Excrements" (qumâmah) is a
distortion of 'Church of the Resurrection' (qiyâmah).

Editorial note to the edition

Nor till thy fall could mortals guess
Ambition's less than littleness!

BYRON,
"Ode to Napoleon Bonaparte"

Having exalted himself into the chair of wisdom, he
tells us much that every man knows, and much that
he does not know himself.

SAMUEL JOHNSON
Life of Pope

The Delphic injunction hasn't guided my life. From fear, laziness, stupidity, decorum or prevision of boredom, I haven't spent much time getting to know myself. As for expressing myself, that's another matter. This section explores that in essays and delivers some oblique self-presentations in poems, journal excerpts, interviews, and some odd bits of prose. If it's not the de luxe tour of the dark interior, it's all I plan to offer. The company motto is By Indirection Find Direction Out.

Two Iowan Baudelaires
Sweating Out Tetrameters

ON JUSTICE, whom I'd met at Chapel Hill in 1944, was at the Iowa City station with Tom Rogers and a blue Ford. The heat was a phenomenon, brilliantined, gloomy, masterful. And Iowa City was *ugggly*. I'd been living off Occupation Fat in Heidelberg, Versailles, and Frankfurt, had saved thirty-five hundred dollars teaching soldiers how to read in the Knucklehead School at Frankfurt and, despite pregnant wife and year-old son, thought myself rich.

That first Iowa week I lived *chez* Justice on a mattress of porcupine and iron surrounded by Bacon-wrote-Shakespeare books. (The landlord was the Baconian T. J. Looney's Iowan ego.) I went to class, hunted for an apartment, and angered the Justices—who'd laid out my welcome—by saying "I can't take it. I'm too old and it's too hot. I'll sell insurance."

I stayed. We lived on the second floor of the ugggliest house west of the Mississippi, a shingled cube that listed in the breeze. The baby's first word was "Moke," from the fire that burst out in his roof-slanted bedroom: God's judgment on this esthetic hell. (Though thanks to Him, no casualties.)

One got used to Iowa City, then addicted to it: the workshop stories in blue duplicates, everybody speaking out (*out* of their literary minds). "How can a Harvard prof dribble orange juice on his collar?" asked one workshopper about my first workshopped story.

Dee Snodgrass, Herb Wilner, Justice, Rogers (though he

was mostly up the hill in Academy Land), Don Petersen, Paul Engle (gone most of my two years), Ray West, Cal Lowell, Karl Shapiro. Good company. Every afternoon at four, Justice, Petersen, Rogers, and I played ferocious croquet by the river. Meanwhile, a few of us were deciding that the James-Lubbock-Brooks-Warren-Tate notion of the perfected story was finished. "Break the windows, open the doors. Air." Yet *Augie March* looked too crude for some—"What a style!" *We* knew it was time to take off Flaubert's corset. And to throw away Joyce's glue, shears, and colored markers.

We weren't much *in the world*. Though when the Army-McCarthy hearings brought public swinery into the new quasi-fictional intensity of the tube, we were in the front row of the Union, booing, groaning. Overcome with Event. (Ten years later, babies would devour more event with their pablum.)

My two Iowa years—1952–54—were big for poets. There was much translating, sestina-writing, debate about meters. Lowell taught Five Lyric Poets (mistranslating Horace, Chénier, and Rilke before discovering you could cover gorgeous mistakes by calling them "Imitations"); he and Gerald Else taught non-Greekists the *Iliad*—in Greek (I remember only Μῆνιν ἄειδε, θεά, Πηληϊάδεω Ἀχιλῆος, and maybe not that); Tate and Gordon came in (separately) to wow us with literary charm, we read *Beowulf* and Middle English (passing annotated texts to each other), flipped through two hundred books a week to pass the Ph.D. orals, partied, wrote, worked on the *Western Review* (it published grand stuff in those years), seldom left Iowa City.

Ph.D. writers were new then, giving jobs to them was new, but it began, and I suppose most of us were lucky, spending only a few years in the swamps of freshman English. These were the years of Ike's Great Tranquility. We had babies by the carload. So it wasn't just getting up the rent (the few bachelors survived on a Calcutta beggar's income), it was getting bread, milk, jello, and diaper-service money into the till. We went to the MLA bazaar, the only road to the well-filled trough. No one went off to Canadian woods, to Paris or Washington. Bill Belvin (the poet who'd been our diaper man) worked in a body shop but was fired for being too deliberate; he was also too deliberate for freshman English and the diaper service. The rest of us more exploded than graded our freshman essays.

White paper sat in our typewriter carriages: our Ithacas.

Of course, retrospect lays gold on the two years. Rilke, Rimbaud, Donne, and our own poems and stories. No war, no Watergate. When Snodgrass and I met over family leftovers in the Quonset Village garbage house, lyric fragrance veiled the odors. Some Rilke poems can never be read without that stale ground bass.

I was happy to leave (two years to the day—June 11, 1954—since the Rock Island Rocket dumped me there) and didn't go back for eighteen years.

In July 1972 Iowa City still had the look of careless fixity. There was the same brilliantine heat gleaming on the river, the Old Capitol, the fraternity houses. It was between semesters, there was no one around, it was like the great American photographs of midwestern desolation. "How could you have loved it?" asked my companion.

"It?"

No, not *it*; *them*! My pals, my poet-and-story-writing pals. Poems counted, stories counted, people read the way they ate and drank. At croquet, poets. At the garbage house, poets. In class, poets. Almost all pals. Not bad.

"Don't judge the place by the place."

Sestina at Thirty-Two

Thirty-two's a good year to celebrate
In verse: a modestly large number
Which hardly ruffles you
After the disaster of thirty.
The problem's finding an honest subject,
One that will touch but not excite the heart.

For of course it's now that the heart
Reminds you you'd better celebrate;
It's life's-past eight, and a fair number
Of claques are waiting to cheer you,
Ones you couldn't afford before you were thirty.
Most of them are, naturally, subject

To economic conversions of object to subject
By small unmusical pressures on their heart.
(As drunken soldiers celebrate
The end of a siege, they number
Ten thousand torches on the walls.) You,
Aflame from thirty, at thirty-

Two find your rear end crisped, those thirty
years of sneaky discretion the subject
of epitaphs, tears, sermons.
                              The heart
of the matter's this: don't celebrate
A single occasion. Wait till a number
pile up, then crow, "Oh me, oh you."

The reporters scribble "thirty"
Under stories only after the subject's
Pumped by hows, whens, whys. A rose's heart
Is even trickier: to celebrate
it, you must praise all of it; to number
it, you must un-rose it.
                    So you

don't. What you do is you
don't. That's the formula for thirty-
two.
        So, love, there's your subject,
fit for old Shahs.
                    Valete, dear heart
We'll move on together, celebrate
ensemble.
            "Did you hear? His number's
Up."

        "Thirty-two."
                    So young for you,
So almost heart-shaped a number,
So uncelebrated an unsubject.

These excerpts from journals (kept erratically for more than thirty years) roughly center about the middle-class Western notion of individuality. The individuals are people of artistic and scientific accomplishment. Center stage, though, is the père de famille—*fantasist-observer-gossip-lover-note-taker-instructor-fiction-writer-closet-narcissist.*

Journal

October 28, 1958

Frank Lloyd Wright here for *Chicago Review*. Mandel Hall filled, crowd stood for Wright, elegant in blue suit, blue handkerchief flowering from pocket. Priestly poet. Speech rambling, moving: for Jeffersonian *aristoi*, buildings sign of "art"; Americans "who believe only what they can touch," not up to this state any more; witness the Robie House—the first house to mark America's artistic independence. It's there *they* have to have a dormitory.

Afterwards, I trail him round the Robie House, asking "why the open square" between the two rooms: "To bring them together. There was a piece of classical sculpture there." There'd been no houses around, the bulbs had "a softer, opalescent" quality. (Critics complain of the darkness in Wright houses. Different standards of light and dark.) "Built to last three hundred years," tapping the oak ribs. Recalled the greenery. "Wonderful plants." (Across the street, the cut-rate Saarinen dorm gloomed whitely. He didn't see it.) Quiet, straightforward, moving. The most touching thing: "You'd never seen brick so beautiful." *

---

* 1981: I pass this house a thousand times a year; its beauty never fails to lift my heart.

November 4, 1958

Katie [Stern]: "I'll never unthink you, Andrew [Stern]."

Story: When MacAllister was young, it was thought that he would have a great future; when he was old it was believed he'd had a great past. There had never been evidence to support either belief. MacAllister had thrown up the most elaborate smokescreen we'd ever seen. . . . (Nietzsche: "Egoism is that law of perspective which makes the immediate seem insurmountable, the distant trivial.")

Story: X could always tell what was happening to Y by reading the company ads. Any time Y wanted to go somewhere, he opened another store. In 19—— there were five of them, and they told the story of what he had been doing for two decades.

January 1, 1958

Christopher [Stern] (after our long New Year's Eve party): "I was kept awake by the dancing—I mean by the records—so I decided to have a little New Year's Eve party of my own. I got a chair and took a cookie and just lied back and relaxed."

February 13, 1958

Story: Young woman, sleeping beside her husband, has dream about being in a smoky room with lot of strangers, feels someone take her hand, without looking, knows it's hand of man she's been falling in love with. (For "The

Making and Breaking of Americans") Get that marvelous moment when one learns that the beloved loves you. Solid marriage becomes the proscenium arch for affairs: the theater has a big hit.

Saul Bellow, taking Wilhelm Reich therapy in his middle thirties, (while writing *Augie M.*), discovered he'd tried to hang himself as a boy. (*Dangling Man* before knowledge.)

Seneca on Augustus: *Clementium non voco lassem crudelitatem.* "I don't call exhausted cruelty clemency." Virtue as depleted vice. (For "The Making and Breaking of Americans")

For love story: At first it's a candle, lit at one end, easily blown out. Then it begins burning at both ends, finally the whole thing's aflame, you're aflame, you're nothing but flame.

At first, the affair is like money in the bank; then an expense; then it's not the wherewithal, it's all, purchase as well as purchasing power. And more than that. It's all currency, all movement, unfixable, unstoppable.

The girl: "Isabel didn't have legitimate emotions." Taking off wedding ring in sleep. (Never has it off.)

Christopher asks if my novel is about a "noveler." (He said to the literary Mrs. Steinbach: "Susie, do you know what a novel is?")

David Riesman at my birthday party: The pillars of Hercules closing the Atlantic to the bursting Phoenicians.

Daughters of Norstadt and Kennan at Connecticut College. Suppose Kennan and Acheson's daughters—or any daughters of distinguished men who are enemies on front page—become friends. Oh yes, Juliet and Romela.

Robert Lowell talking about the competition to make the best desserts. Describing the manic bursts in his head.

Katie and Chris trading baseball cards. Katie: "I gave him McDougall for the baddest player." Chris: "She choosed it." Gay [Stern]: "Chose it." Katie: "I don't even know the names." Chris: "Either do I." Katie: "*You knew McDougall.*" (Chris's favorite player: "Anus Slaughter")

March 12, 1958

Story: If you were to hear an account of X's actions, his deeds, his *x*'s, his *y*'s, you would believe him to be a saint. He was not, however, even a good man, and five minutes in his presence convinced you of it. Goodness consists in some proportion between kind feeling and useful action; it shows itself gracefully. Y was tense with his responsibility toward goodness; his expressions were almost never right as he censured the malicious and praised the good. Still he was a terrier about his notions—certain, severe, fierce. "Suffering makes room in the soul. Jews can suffer, know how to suffer. That's why it's their tune." (The Chosen People in a parlor outlining the place of love, suffering, feeling, and personality.)

Z is a wild garden full of flowers spaced in rock nooks and shrubbery. X raises the greatest jonquils in the world, weeding, manuring, watering with a marvelously productive ferocity.

October 1960

Andrew (pointing his rifle at Gay): "Put up yours hands." (Gay puts them up. She's sitting on a bar stool.) Andrew: "Don't get off yours horse."

Andrew ends his list of friends: "And I'm a friend of me."

Katie giving me violin lessons. I contrast her sweet pedagogy with my harsh attempts to teach Christopher French. Penitent, I tell him I wish I brought him more happiness. Christopher: "Oh, you bring me happiness." I: "Well, I hope you'll remember me with love." Christopher: "I don't know if I'll remember you with love, but I'll sure remember you."

October 31, 1960

Andrew confusing the Halloween "We want candy" with "We want Kennedy."

December 22, 1960

Andrew: "There's a hole in the sky where the plane lives."

May 1961

Moksie [Chris] (after being twitted about his *amour-propre*): "I can't get along without myself."

July 25, 1961

Explaining Ulysses' speech about the "specialty of rule," then, at Katie's insistence, reading it. After five lines, Katie sighs and says, "Whew, those Greeks sure were smart."

August 24, 1961

Christopher made Virginia [Heiserman] a birthday card with the motto Growing Old Should Be an Everyday Passion, but was worried about the use of *passion*. I told him it was not used right, that the correct word was *feeling*. He said that he just loved the word *passion* and almost never had an opportunity to use it.

December 1961

Andrew said he couldn't lift something because his arms were drunk. (Like Luzzie's foot-asleep description: "There are bees in my foot." On Halloween Luzzie [Heiserman] went around collecting; back home, he looked by mistake at Virginia's pound of string beans. "Is dis all I got?" Alison [Heiserman] (January 1962) debunking for Luz's sake: "Santa Claus is just Christmas dressed up like a man.")

June 24, 1962

In the third-floor waiting room of Alitalia a mob scene. We hear that five hundred sandwiches have been consumed: "The relatives are eating." There were six relatives per customer (seven for the six Sterns); the terminal was Little Italy. Gay: "Now we don't have to go." (*A Rébours.*) In back of our domestic rectangle, an old man who looked as if he should have been in an underwear top was betting on take-off time. Eight nine-year-olds tried to con me out of lollipops. (Grandpa Clark distributed the last one, discarded—by Andrew—and married to a piece of napkin. The recipient of this Point Four operation flung it into the trash can: "It's wet." Grandpa hurt at the rejection.) The marche funèbre downstairs, relatives dropping away to sobs, cries, moans, "*Ciao, bella. Ciao, carina.*" Boarding, blue lights gashing the dark, the relatives like fish behind airport glass. Katie thought one was supposed to wave at unfortunate nontravelers; princesslike, she waved.

Naturally—the Italian adverb—we'd been put in the wrong seats: no room for Nicky's crib. A stewardess passed out candies, slipper-socks, magazines, American newspapers (no Italian ones—disappointing the priest). We waited; we roasted. Gay: "There's no substitute for flying." At eleven or so, we took off; I was tired, dirty, hot, nauseous, Nick-ridden (he was in my arms the whole trip).

Another delight: my seat was a non-recliner. I ate with left hand—and I mean hand—while Christopher supported Nick's head. Such nights do not make shipmates of us all. Two A.M., Katie spotted the sun coming out of Europe with innocent malice.

Rome in heat; nothing new for Chicagoans. Counterparts of the farewell-relatives on the observation ramp. A cabbie took our bags, piled them on his Fiat 600, omitting Andrew's, which, five hours later, he brought to the *pensione*. Around the airport, Floridian foliage and a great-nosed statue of Leonardo. The twenty kilometers to Rome are splendid, enough carved stone to remind us why we came.

In every ruin, the solitary, augustan cat. Few dogs. Hunchbacks and little people.

Grass dry and prickly. The defeat of Roman planning. The carnality of marble.

July 3, 1962

Pensione Scaligera. Personnel: The Roches (pronounced "Roaches") eighty-four and eighty, a tiny Chinese couple, refugees (seven years ago) from Shanghai prosperity. For thirty-eight years, Mr. R. was bookkeeper for a German indigo firm; he went to English schools, cannot read or write Chinese. Mme. R. is the daughter of a Spaniard and a Chinese. Their English is grammatical, careful, littered with inelegance: "big shot" (emphasis on the final consonants); "the kids." Avaricious, decent. They shipped twenty-three cases of goods from Shanghai thanks to their son-in-law, an Italian big shot in Chinese Customs. Son-in-law died of an enlarged heart several years ago leaving Loretta, a girl who at age twelve carries fifty-seven kilos (126 pounds) and is consumed by love-hate for her little sister Christina, her Chinese grandparents, and her pretty Momma. Her English is a surer version of her grandmother's, liberally stoked with harsh abruptness. Momma is the property of the ex-Major of Mines and Fortifications, Signor Buschi—originally French, great-grandpère being a Napoleonic officer who brought his English wife here in N's campaign. The Major was in Libya before the war, then, called up, he was the eighth prisoner of war captured. It was November 8, a "lucky day," because he'd been eighth in his class at the college. Long face, loose tie, open collar, phlegmatic speech, knowledgeable, vain, no English, enjoys bookkeeping and the pleasures of the Pensione (including Signora Toscani). Most of the guests are English-speaking members of FAO (Food and Agricultural Organization).

Newspapers: *Il Messagero* (government); *Pase Sera* (Communist); *La Stampa* (Fiat); *Il Giorno d'Italia* (*destra*); *Corriere della Sera* (*Le Monde*).

Story: "En route from San Pietro in Vincoli to San Giovanni Laterano, William Boris had the following encounter: Standing by a woman whose loose breasts had gripped his heart, he found the pressure of his leg on hers returned. Inflamed, excited, erect, he dismounted three stops before San Giovanni . . ." Or is his tourist passion so strong he doesn't follow her off the bus? "I'll take the bus tomorrow." After all, San Giovanni was a sure thing. That night, sleeping next to his menstruating wife . . .

San Giovanni filled with German priests: "As Walter von der Vogelweide—of whom some of you may have heard—said, 'Innocent the Third was too young.'"

July 15, 1962

Local ethics: The newspapers' sympathetic, novelistic accounts of murders (the workman who knocked off his *padrone*'s head). "*Questa non era bella*," said the judge (about the killer knocking over a child as he ran downstairs). A curator wanted to fire a janitor who'd stolen "only the very little pictures." A Roman woman's response to moral dilemmas: "Aren't I making love well?"

At John Brown's apartment in the Palazzo Lancelotti (two Lancelotti still live there), a cradle of orange stone,

loggia, statues, marble medallions, fountain, chirping bird-
ies. The "presentation" of Harold Rosenberg's book on
Gorki by Professor Argan.[†] Two beautiful women, one
of whom stretched her beautiful legs in front of mine, a
refined, creamy, substantial—yet ungross—blonde, liquid
and marvelous to contemplate; and a beautiful brunette
art dealer who gave me her card. Paolo Milano introduced
me as "the famous author of *Golk*." Signora Brown and
my publisher were the only ones who'd heard of it. The
former poured me the equivalent of four jiggers of gin.

November 12, 1962

Venice: Katie thinks in Italian now, phrases she over-
hears on the *vaporetto*. *"Perch' no parl' a tu frateya?"*
"Cosi vuio ci-ci?" The *vaporetto* passengers are always the
same. There's a grandmother "delivering her child," "two
pretty people at Redentore who always stand in the same
place. There's a man who always calls me *amore*."

Sergio's account of Mario Praz's speech "On the New
American Novel," in which thirty minutes were spent de-
nouncing new films and film makers who had not paid
Praz sufficient homage; he built five brilliant bridges back
to the subject.

November 26, 1962

Saw Ezra Pound[‡] holed up with companion Olga Rudge
in Calle Querini, one *campo* away from the Salute. He was

[†] 1980. For several years now, the Communist mayor of Rome.
[‡] The small differences between this book's versions of the same incidents may
interest its readers.

under blankets, seemed small, eyes very small, bright blue, voice, too, under wraps, but a beautiful Celtic burr in its American fuzz. He says he thinks of work about five minutes a day. Came to Venice in 1902, three days after the Campanile fell. Miss Rudge says he reads aloud, the *Paradiso*, a book on microorganisms ("beyond me"). I relayed Hugh Kenner's relay of Louis Zukofsky's request for his letters. Pound smiled, perhaps at all good Jews getting together. Miss Rudge asked Ezra if she could give Andrew one of the birthday sweets, initialed candied fruit. After long silence, slow consent.

December 10, 1962

Andrew recounted story of that famous woman Maria who asked all these people to let her and Giuseppi stay on a sofa, but they were bad and made them go into a barn. Andrew drew a picture of it, but goofed because Domenica pushed his arm. (This is the pretty girl who sits next to him in the desk room.) It took me a while to realize he was telling the Christmas story.

The monsignor from Trieste strode off the train from the Vatican Council meetings with his heavy bag, waved off the little *facchino* ("You'll have to get two or three bowls of tripe in you before you can lift it off the ground, son"), and, followed by the Darbs, a family of charity workers, went into the Terminus Hotel and asked for a dozen glasses. "But there are only nine of you, Monsignor." "Bring a dozen." He dropped into a chair and brought from his cape two liters of white wine.

Signora Lydia's five-year-old, sick and *sotto sviluppato*, is being sent—free—to the mountains.

December 12, 1962

If E. P. is insane, God help the rest of us. A terrific two-and-a-half hour tea with him and Miss Rudge. He was extraordinarily scrupulous, deliberate, tactful, assertive without meanness, full of self-deprecation. He talked of "Henry" (James), whom he "saw on rare occasions" and "Hem." ("I always *thought* he was Catholic.") The anecdotes were extracted by me as if from a set of old teeth. "Frost wanted to be New England." "There's a coherence in both Frost and Eliot." "Don't think pianos waited for the railroad." He smokes three cigarettes a month. Describing Wyndham Lewis's gradual blindness: "He drew while he could still see something." In *Villon*, he was trying to get tunes which went with the poems. He and Rudge went to see the movie *Seven Deadly Sins*; he was bored, but, four months later, remembered the "greed" episode.

January 3, 1963

Pound opened the door, shook hands. Stern: "How are you?" Pound: "Old, senile." Stern: "Nonsense." Pound: !

We sat in the first floor room, spoke of the *Paris Review* interview. "Your letter to Can Grande?" "I did want to set a few things straight." He seemed to be having difficulty with his memory, head wrinkled, twisted, clutched. After an hour and a half, I got up and he, relieved, rose, smiled, and went upstairs. He was very noisy, a piece of plaster fell on an ashtray as Olga Rudge and I talked. (He'd been rather curt with her.)

Christopher—who's reading *Arrowsmith*—said, as we walked to Ca' Foscari to find *David Copperfield* in the seminar library, "I never realized that love was so much before. You know, that it would be so important for a man. Like in the book, he wants to give this nineteen-year-old girl a kiss so much; she's got such round lips."

January 6, 1963

"Silent Night" in the Siena Cathedral.

Story of a nice man who's known as the man who tortured someone like Hemingway. (Hemingway begged Philip Young not to publish his book: "It'll hold me up for six months." "Don't read it," said Young, suspending those analytic powers which enabled him to see that Hemingway would have to read it.)

Story: Sees his old love in a dream talking with her husband, knows they never talk, yet tries to read their lips.

At school yesterday—Katie reported—Sore (Suora) Emmanuele went on about the beautiful parts of flowers while little Marina muttered her "*Mama mia, Madre.*" Marina likes to say "*Anch' io ho fatto così.*" But she *hasn't done it* at all and keeps getting zero. Luccio was told he wasn't fit for fourth grade, though he claims he's read everything. When Christopher asked him, "What, for instance?" Luccio said, "*The Encyclopedia.*" When Christopher tried to tell him what he was reading, Luccio's response was, "*Muio, muio, muio, muio.*" And "Push off." Luccio stays away from school on "flower-bringing days."

Last night's fog had Kate, Christopher and me running back and forth between the Zattere and San Zaccharia for the *traghetto*. Horns were blowing in the lagoons, visibility about fifteen feet.

Nicky's first two words: "*due*" and "*ciao*." Just now, trailing Nera on her semiarboreal course from bureau to desk and back, he was drawn into "Ne-ah."

An American physics student from Padua showed up yesterday, boasted about spending three "terrific" months with a Yugoslavian girl. His half-suppressed vanity and wildness made him dangerous; he devoured three-fifths of our chicken. He has a diagram of elementary particles and sang a kind of technical praise song about Dirac (who predicted antimatter).

Cici: Cici paid taxes twice rather than acknowledge that he changed his name from Francesco. He tried to get a driving license for his new motor boat. Otto rehearsed him for a month, but it didn't work. The commissioner asked, "What do you do in the fog when you hear two toots?" Cici, flushed and sweating, said, "*Niente*." "What was that?" Cici repeated, "Nothing." "What do you mean 'nothing'?" Cici: "I won't take it out when there's fog."

A rich American girl with a dog came to the pensione. Cici adores them both. The girl said the dog could eat rice. Cici brought the dog the rice with his own hands; there was a spoon in the dish.

A letter came to Mrs. Cici under her maiden name. Cici searched for hours in the register until Otto told him who it was.

He is not a good judge of class. People in suits turn out to be workers from the south, those in turtlenecks and track shoes British lords. So many foreign pederasts hide out in Cici's that he began to think that the whole aristocracy is queer. "It must be the correct thing." He finds it impossible to use the phone directory since it is in Italian, not dialect. He looked up *oculista* under *C* for *culista*. Said Otto, "What do eyeglasses have to do with the *cula* [rear end]?" He looked up American Express under Merican. Cici is fond of saying *mettimo* [*mettiamo*] *in casa* ["take for instance"], but he never does get to the point. He reads only headlines. During the Suez Canal crisis, he asked resentfully why they never wrote about "the canals around here."

Stern: How did you get to Agassiz? Pound: Through von Humboldt. (He either didn't know or had forgotten that Agassiz opposed Darwin.)

This is the coldest winter since 1929, when you could walk from the Giudecca to San Michele. Coal is running low, but there's always noon sun on the Zattere. Men chip at ice on the *campi*, and the *gabioni* [gulls] mutter near the piers. The pigeons, fed twice a day by the city, are not getting the usual tourist handout; they're in a frenzy at feeding time. The cats, too, seem to be hiding out.

January 30, 1963

Gay and I went to E. P.'s for tea. He was upstairs on the third floor in bed but disinclined to accept Miss Rudge's climate excuse (she kept talking about hibernation). He was ashamed not to be up, ashamed to meet Gay with only his sweater on and under the blankets. He flung the blanket over his bare feet. There was a fire in the raised Venetian fireplace, translucent plastic sheets over skylight and windows. Miss Rudge said she'd bought the house in 1929. To him: "You were lounging on the Riviera. You came down in April, I think." He has a cold and she called his doctor in Rapallo, who counseled aspirin. Her thumb is split, she stokes coal at midnight. "Domestic detail bores you, Ezra, doesn't it?" "No, you take care of it, Olga." He pronounces her name with the full "Ol." I borrowed his translation of *Women of Trachis*. Pound: "Precious little Sophocles there." Stern: "Tried any others?" Pound: "I was interested in the *Agamemnon*." He muttered something about coherence. A huge smile for Gay's farewell.

Sergio [Perosa] told me about Professor Cellini. Cellini claims Olivier and Gielgud don't understand Shakespeare: "They have no right to act." Sergio went with him to the record store in Via 22 Marzo. Cellini asked for a record player that would play only words, not music; he needed it for the *seminario*. He claims to be an actor, a mountain climber and "though I can't read music," a composer. He ridiculed the concert repertory, though he hasn't been to a recital in three years. At lunch he flirts with a cross-eyed, frightened Professoressa d'Arabo.

February 19, 1963

Met Mary de Rachewiltz (Pound's daughter), a down-to-earth person, fair-haired and moon-cheeked, just back from America, where everything is wonderful, especially Gothic Yale where they have "experts for everything." "You get used to going into a cathedral to take a bath."

Said her mother, "*La Catédrale engloutie.*" She saw Frost the day before his death, he seemed fine. She invited us to their castle: "Children enjoy it anyway." And especially invited Katie for her daughter's thirteenth birthday next week. "She acts like ten, doesn't want to grow up." She finds her father a bit difficult so she asks me the meaning of "throwing the baby out with the bath." I pass the question to him. De Rachewiltz: "I'll never learn, then." Poor E. P. droops. Mr. Stoppani [the American consul] told me she put "father unknown" on her passport. Miss Rudge told me about *her* life, her grandfather, a gentleman farmer who took a flock of sheep to Youngstown, Ohio, became a Catholic, and was ostracized. His children had to be sent away to school. The girls entered convents. Her father went to England and married an Irish girl, a singer. Miss Rudge left Youngstown early, at nine, went to school in England, at thirteen, France. She went back to the U.S. for her parents' fiftieth wedding anniversary.

Another visitor is Giancarlo Ivancich, a friend of Hemingway's. His family has been in Venice since the fall of the republic, they own the Grand Hotel. Hemingway fell in love with his sister Adriana. (*Across the River and into the Trees.*) I went back to his gloomy *palazzo* behind San Marco. He showed me pictures of Hemingway and read from a children's story Hemingway wrote for Adriana's child: "'Have a bite of Hindu Trader,' offered the lion." He was at Hemingway's funeral. There's an inscription of Hemingway's on the proofs—"*Finca Vigia*—the poor man's *Duino.*"

February 27, 1963

Took Joan [FitzGerald] (back from States) to Pound's.
Four of us had tea upstairs. Usual creaky talk. Joan said I
was having dinner at Goofyheims. "Yes," I said, "She re-
members playing tennis with you [Pound] years ago." He
sat up in bed. He had to thank me for becoming incredible,
had been worried about not remembering. "Fifty-three per
cent fiction." (*In Any Case* on his reading table.) Chill.
Anger. The two women made a bit more talk, went downstairs. I debated leaving without goodby, instead, went over
to the bed, shook hands and said, "You're right. Most talk
is 90 percent guff." He pulled me down to inches of his
old face. "No, no. I never recognize benevolence. Wrong,
wrong, wrong. 87 percent wrong." I said, "You've made
your mistakes, but those who like pinning them on you
aren't in your class." Pound: "You don't know what it's
like, not to be able to see good will. Not able to remember." He'd left only "scattered notes," never got anything
right. I said I'd been reading *Mauberley*, it was right on
target. Pound: "Once you get on the wrong track . . ."
And something Italian—Dante?—about perfection, most
of it left in his beard. All the time he held hard to me,
looking through, beyond. Stating his case? Asking judgment? Forgiveness? Close to tears; I should have stayed,
but disengaged, patted his hand for goodbye.

March 1963

The restorer of the Veronese in San Sebastiano has his
own Venetian daubs propped up on the scaffold, relaxes
with them after a session on the walls. His partners work

on the Giottos in Padua and the Paolo della Francescas in Arezzo. Liselotte [Höhs] invited him to look at her not dissimilar Venice vistas.

We walked with Joan and Otto to Malamocco, its campanile hiding-and-seeking in the mist. Football—Croatian style—above the dunes, Jon [Levy], Christopher, and Andy working out fancy plays, then ate thin veal while old fellows rolled *bocce*; a dusty walk to Alberoni, and a slow ride back over the slick folds of the lagoon.

Andrew's Naming of Us: Christopher, The Starter (of fights); Katie, The Screamer; Andrew, The Fighter; Daddy, The Wanter (Blake's "I want, I want"? No.); Mommy, The Nicest. In bed, he listens to the *Scuola Elementare* story on his transistor.

Signora Lydia's husband, lungs burned out in the glass factory, had his pension application *respinto*. Signora L. must go to Mestre to appeal, is afraid to go to mainland while the weather's bad. (The old signora in the courtyard hasn't been across to San Marco for years.)

Venetians: The two "duchesses," kleptomaniacal jewel thieves, dressing à la 1890, all yellow, all purple, mistresses of kings, daughter of one married to a Guinness. One lives in a palazzo, the other Abbey St. Gregorie. They speak "perfect French." Born in Naples, one sang before King Umberto, he called her "Duchess" and she "became" one. (What else is a duchess?) They take the mud baths in the Brenta, hoist their dresses, to show me their livid old gams. "What do you think of that?" Every afternoon they entertain Venetian and foreign dregs at Harry's Bar. I go for inspection. They refuse to credit that I'm from Chicago. "I will see you in New York." "I live in Chicago." "We will meet in the Parc Centrale." They drink hot tea. One lifts the tea cup close to her nose. Some of the nose melts and falls into the cup. She drinks it. "In Paris I spend all my time with Victor Hugo. I never miss a weekend." Explanation: she goes to the Hugo house in Place de Vosges and communes with the books and furniture.

Doctor and Mrs. G. He is a professor of dentistry, a bloodsucker, has bought a mountain in the Dolomites, constructed a house in V——. There is a blind son—who lives in the YMCA—a daughter married to a Turkish salesman, another son, "a genius," who lives in Otto's pension and is starving to death because they won't let him eat "between meals." They gave up drinking wine, so as not to have to supply it to workers. Once they invited Joan for coffee; she also had an orange and there were uneasy jokes about the extra fifteen lire.

Joan made a terracotta head of the daughter of a Chicago executive. The mother said, "This girl has always rubbed me the wrong way." (The girl is nine years old.) A few years later, a friend of Joan's tried to rent the head for an exhibition. It had been smashed, the $250 insurance collected.

December 21, 1963

Between the Miracoli and San Zanipolo two shepherds play a bagpipe and a miniature oboe; melancholy, spirited music. Dressed in wool cloaks, feet in straps and wool. They come every Christmas season for holiday money.

Kate's distinction: Mommy was not a person who finds things, but a person who knows where things are. (The troubadour and the jongleur.)

July 1963

Cambridge (England): Tallish, slender, stoop-shouldered fellow with a cape of thin white hair came to our door with letter that had been misdelivered to his place across the street. (They'd "had a man named Stein" staying with them.) Turned out that this fellow—who looks like a failed draper or like Mr. Brittain, the little English watchmaker whose shop was on Columbus Avenue in the thirties—is "Prof" Dirac. I get in the habit of going over to talk with him in the afternoons. (In the mornings, he works on physics.) Sometimes he's squeezing apple segments through gauze into a bowl: "Making apple jelly." I ask him if he visualizes his mathematic cosmology, and he says that yes, often, pictures do come. He gives me his recent article from *Scientific American*, which is a very clear and rather exciting critique of relativity theory; I give him a paperback *Golk* (just out in Penguin). In his living room, there's a picture of a black-haired, becaped young Dirac in full stride. I suppose when he was earning his Nobel, he was a physical as well as a mental Byron. He appears to relish talking—I later learn he's renowned for silence—and talks with that dry concision which is the sound of intellectual music in mine ears. A "big-bang man," he makes me think that theory has as much to do with religious hunger as rational analysis. (He is, I believe, *croyant*.) There's a crew of American physicists on the street. One of them told me that he's the only one of the lot who's so much as *heard* of Dirac, that the others are not only experimental types but illiterate. He says the *Scientific American* article contains the only new theoretical ideas he's heard in three years in Cambridge. (The hoggish American physicist who visited us in Venice was, then, a rarity; I wish he'd been even rarer.)

August 1963

Party for Lowell at Faber and Faber. Yesterday, Lowell had given me an issue of the *New York Review of Books* which came out during the New York newspaper strike. He says it's the best thing that's happened in letters in years. The party: Bill Alfred, with a beautiful English girl; Empson, Chinese-bearded; Richards and wife; Louis Mac-Neice,* elegant, a trifle weary, recommending I go see the little church near the Tower of London (St. Pancras?) which has Roman pavement and a model of "Boadicea's London."

February 14–15, 1965

Chicago: Auden in little room at Quad Club puttering in slippers, a granny manner, but no granny. A frightful, plowed, pitted face. No bathtub, and no drink till five: "I thought it was a club." He had his own gin and drank it warm in a papercup. Alienation? "I have friends, I have never felt alienated. What does it mean, anyway? Old people in hotel lobbies?"

"Good poets who are bad men? I know three, Yeats, Brecht, and Yevtushenko" (though he doesn't think he's much of a poet). They're all "pure shit. Just shit. Yeats was vain, Brecht terrible to women. He'd have them scrubbing floors in ten minutes." "Dear MacNeice always had diffi-

* MacNeice died a few weeks later.

cult women. At the end, he found a wonderful one. Then he got his feet wet, drank whiskey, and died." Stravinsky needs his bottle of whiskey a day, he and "dear Eliot" are "terrible hypos" (chondriacs). "I have the thickest blood." Auden from *odin*, Icelandic for "disciple." Spain wasn't quite the last fling with politics. "They didn't have anything for me to do. I went from Valencia to Barcelona, but there was nothing to do. So I left." "I suppose it was the Nazi-Soviet pact that opened my eyes." His St. Mark's Place house is the one in which Trotsky edited *Novy Mir* in 1914–15: "There should be a plaque." He came here in January '39. One brother, now with FAO, went to India as a geologist, another farmed a while in Canada. In the general strike of '26 he drove cars for the Trade Union Congress, once took Tawney to Mecklinburg Square, then went to see a cousin who threw him out of the house. "All it was was love of driving cars, buses, trains." Pound didn't get accent of *Seafarer* right, didn't see double accent. "If you do something like that, you should do it right." Much on money and his tours. "I'll spend my sixtieth birthday in a few weeks alone in an Oregon motel." Religious poetry hard. In fact, it was hard to tell the truth "and it doesn't get easier. Yet I never write what I don't feel. All right, a sonnet to Miss Smith. You can substitute Miss Jones, but you really can't substitute Buddha for Christ."

Much distance between the mind of the poems—those that saved my sanity when I worked for the department store in '47—and the mind of the man. The Granny-wrapping protects the old fellow. Saul: "Perhaps he needs old age." He certainly reaches for it. Auden told Art [Heiserman] he reads only medieval poetry for pleasure, he [Auden] should look hard at medieval and classical rhetoric.

Where's the old-maid meanness in the fellow? Except for bitchiness about the bad poets (all hard on women), it didn't come out. In his slippers, head bent, he tried to push the car out of the icy grooves. Next day, his first question was "Did you get the car out?" He'd come into the Quad Club, no one looked at him, he got a table and looked very much alone. I took my coffee over to him, "May I?" "Thank you so much," he said. He doesn't say goodbye.

October 1965

"*Sono demoralizatto.*" Bald old fellow in exhausted gray suit coat and pants split at the fly. We're en route to Siena, he's getting off at Monteriggioni to peddle "this junk"— *questa roba*—a paper sack of damaged fruit knives, peelers, screws. Looking out the window: "It's good land." *Le vigne, le vigne.* He's had terrible times. As for the government: "Those Eaters. *Mangiatori, tutti.*" He lives on a tiny war pension, and peddling. What *soddisfazione* can come from such work, he sees nothing that counts (a harsh look at the sack). There is a connection between the endowed soil of Tuscany and his own misery: *he* has not had *buona fortuna*, is not blessed like this vine-bright earth. His soil was ready, but there was no rain, no sun; his cultivation was for nothing. He counted over the twelve towns between Empoli (where I got on) and Siena, ticking them off on lumpy fingers. At Monteriggioni, he didn't budge. It didn't matter where he got off. He hadn't made his pitch yet. Then on with his blasted, colorless fedora: "I have no money." I gave him eight hundred lire. In two seconds, he was jaunty (visions of pasta, wine), he shook hands, and got down his cursed sack. I watched him walk down the white street of Castelleno-in-Chianti.

Lunch with Ezra Pound, Olga Rudge, and Joan. Much fussing about his food. "Is the fish good, Ezra?" "No." At

Joan's I gave him a snort of scotch. He swaggered, then drank up. Olga went off. He grew confused. "I shouldn't have let Olga go." In the middle of nothing: "I don't see it." (Joan thought he meant cut-out sculpture, a subject talked about an hour earlier.)

A gondola ride—first in years—to his favorite places. He insisted Olga take the comfortable seat. She: "'They will come no more/The old men with beautiful manners.'" I told him about the latest crop of Hyde Park Corner speakers, Pakistanis and Indians pointing umbrellas at each others' chests: "'But you are no gentleman, sir. No gentleman. I will skewer you, sir. I will skewer your guts.'" Pound: One of the funniest things I heard at Hyde Park Corner was from an atheist. (Imitating Cockney): "'They say 'ell 'as walls of brass a thousand miles 'igh and five miles thick. What hi wants to know his *'ow they get hin!'*" He and Olga off to Paris, she's worried about appropriate presents. Pound: "I believe glass and lace handkerchiefs are expected." Of an ever-transitory English publisher: "A rogue and a charlatan." In his great tan overcoat, soft checked fedora, swinging his knobby stick, Pound still cuts a swath.

March 1966

Chicago: Andrew at breakfast after Nicky said he'd dreamed of a table which walked: "You can imagine skyscrapers wanting to lie down or chairs wanting to get up."

Domestic warfare over the invitations, or rather, the invitation-process to Kate's party. Should anyone be able to ask anyone, or should there be a determined number, a fixed list of names? (The latter was chosen, but it didn't matter, and I had to descend from my post on the second floor to patrol for cigarettes stamped out on floor and excessive nuzzling. A policeman's lot . . .)

In Los Angeles art store, Jeff [Hayden] introduced me to writer Ben Roberts carrying in one of his Grandpa Moses paintings. He's sold a hundred and fifty in two years. He and his writing partner (Ivan Goff) have written for twenty-two years and have "never been congratulated" about a script. He said they construct a "third style." Eva [Marie Saint—Mrs. Hayden] and I watched most of *Raintree County* on television, she remembering when Clift was so drunk he couldn't stand, let alone act.

April 13, 1967

About 4:00 P.M.: Doorbell rang, Andy answered, gun shoved into his chest by slender black with straggly beard about thirty years old. Andy was told to call his mother. Gay came down, holding the wash, managed to keep together, took Andy on her lap (thought the man reacted favorably to that), got him twenty dollars from her purse. Man disappointed, threatened to shoot them, Andy mentioned my wallet upstairs. Gay: "Please don't shoot my son." Went up for wallet, passed Chris and me talking. I noticed she was pale, but I said nothing, kept talking to Chris. She got the few dollars I had—the wallet was on my clothes chest—and went downstairs. More disappointment. The man wanted to take Andy (shield? kidnapping? narcotic confusion?); Gay said, no, he'd be recognized by the neighbors. The fellow left threatening to return if police were told. Gay and Andy came upstairs, collapsed; we called police. Groups of detectives came in all evening (university and city police). Andy remembered the important details (man held gun in left hand), went through the mug books, and picked out a "possible." The next night, more mug books. Uwe Johnson was there; he was astonished at the mug books, the hundreds of black faces, the stories of specialists. ("This one hoists Chevies, this one pours gasoline on girls," etc.)

April 24, 1967

Read *Dossier: Earth* [a play] to about fifty people in the Reynolds Club. Hannah [Arendt] came fifteen minutes late. Bob Lombardo and I went back with her to the *Windermere*. She spoke of emigrating to France, had nothing to do with intellectuals. (Unknown to her, her doctor's thesis on Augustine was known by Marcel, who'd spoken to her after a seminar; she'd also known Aron in Germany). Always managed to read, Joyce in German (1930), Faulkner in French (1934), great moments for her. Worked for a crook who bought and sold railroads, he thought she knew law and could maneuver for him. He proposed to her, she talked of her first husband (Stern) and dodged him. She worked getting children to Palestine, fed them, taught them history, got them papers. Never worked legally, afraid she'd lose the *permis de séjour* if she got the *carte de travail*. Never learned how she got out. In 1940, living in the country, her name was put on cable from America and a messenger—directed by a friend in Marseilles—found her and Heinrich Blucher, now her companion. She got to Marseilles—ingeniously ("one of the awful things is that only the intelligent could survive")—and a boat to Lisbon where the Quakers and Unitarians met her. Her mother came—they gave her a few days in a nice hotel—then America. The shock of English. Was taken in by family as pet European and semi-maid. Their first question: "Do you believe in the Hereafter?" She went upstairs to look up the word in the dictionary. Despair. But she "learned America." They wanted to keep her permanently; she got her mother to send rescue telegram. In New York she continued social work, then got Washington assignment to write briefs (on foreign press?) which became policy.

December 27, 1967

Chicago: About four o'clock went to Cal Lowell's room in the Palmer House. He is sitting in bed in socks, a blue pocket-buttoned shirt, loose tie. Poems, the new "fourteen-liners," are spread and piled on the red quilt. Cal reads ten or twelve of them aloud. The last is about an odd Christmas tree of artificial roses which his daughter was "too unconventional to buy." There were many "annotations"—Harriet [Lowell] calls these "footmarks." He'd written the Christmas tree poem the night before. Since June he's written seventy-four of them. It was after he'd started the lithium treatments. He went in to shave and came out every now and then, face half-mooned with cream. He showed me the bottle of lithium capsules. Another medical gift from Copenhagen. Had I heard what his trouble was? "Salt deficiency." This was the first year in eighteen he hadn't had an attack. There'd been fourteen or fifteen over the past eighteen years. Frightful humiliation and waste. He'd been all set to taxi up to Riverdale five times a week at fifty dollars a session, plus (of course) taxi fare. Now it was a capsule a day and once-a-week therapy. His face seemed smoother, the weight of distress-attacks and anticipation both—gone. He'd lived in "closed communities" since boarding school—Harvard, Kenyon, Black Rock, and the Institution. But the constraints, the dullness of routine, the dullness of the patients. (No wonder his avidity for literary talk.) Madness was like "being in war";

there were some advantages for literature, but the humiliation and the increasing shame were terrible. He'd seen Ezra "since I saw you last." He'd gone to Rapallo in the spring of '65, Ezra had talked wonderfully till Olga came in, and, for the first time, personally, about Olga's violinist hands used for scrubbing. "'I'm living off her income.'" Cal did not feel any egoism in this self-abasement. Pound had held out his hands: "The worm is in them." Later, walking up and down the corridors, trying to find the elevators, Cal got onto Berryman, how he'd had to introduce him twice in one day, and how J.B. kept putting his arm around him till he'd had to tell him he mustn't do that. In connection with one of the poems on the Charles River, he told me for the third or fourth time of the incident that "changed my life." "I struck him [his father] down." (His father had sent an "insolent" letter about a girl in Cal's room to the girl's father.) After Cal knocked him down, he was sent to Merrill Moore. (I said Moore [author of thousands of sonnets] would have been intrigued by the flood of fourteen-liners.) He was off to Mexico City/Cuernavaca at 6:45 the next morning. More meetings like the ones at Caracas which gave him the "blood like rock" poem. He said how hard it was "to rise above things when you're jammed in." Very conscious of physique. When he took off his shirt to shave, he looked in pretty good shape, a bit of a belly, some flab at the hips, but the chest is lean, the arms and shoulders strong. In and out of the bathroom, there was talk of death: "Once you hit fifty it's always on your mind." His talent is best when he's fired up by detail, or by gossip and irony. Generally he dislikes other people's generalities. He's full of Empsonism, always spotting ambiguities. Warm, complicated, edgy. He lay down on the bed in his jacket, and when he got up, took a quick look in the mirror.

Cal's line: "Anyone around who, uh, we know?"

Anniversary Poem

Celibates live longer.
Actuarial Report

I believe the actuaries. My bachelor uncles
and my maiden aunts lived longest, and the strain
of all these years, though tangled with the stress
time everywhere exerts, I do ascribe in no small part
to what succeeded the exchange of what are still called
   vows.

Medical researchers say that one distinguished phase
of union equals running up two flights of stairs;
caution for coronaries. But that expense of spirit
has been budgeted (every state demands its tax).
Lex Julia et Papia Poppaea declared that *caelibes*

Without the sixth degree could not inherit;
vestals were much honored but hard to recruit;
the lamas in Tibet, the monks on Athos
kept even female flies outside the bounds;
the Essenes, the Montanists, the Cathari

Flourished by choice, not flesh, influenced
by Manichean notions of somatic devilry
older than Zoroaster. Saint Pietro
Damiani complained that "lechery
had more legal rights than chastity."

In our more generous time, Lederberg found
bacteria had sex. (And next: particulate lust?)

Marriage is simpler: a mattress, a floor,
a field, a willing, a lack of unwilling.
The ways of love are better paved than love.

Outside the window, by the tulip bed,
twenty-four hundred dollars of exemption plays;
annual song of love. Partner, joint returner,
consider this when Ides bring back the day
that we drank Benedictine on the Rue Verneuil.

Journal

August 23, 1973

Calcutta: Tomorrow this city is 283 years old (if it makes it). The first sight is a surprise, green farmland filling up the bay-broken coast. The airport is large, customs rapid: "You travel light."

Mr. Ghose, the meteorologist, is also* on this flight. "My jeep is meeting me. Can we give you a lift?" There is a driver and a man who fills him in on meteorological matters as we take off. The first living things are cows; and they are also the second and third living things. Skinny white kings, munching, serene; I've never seen cows like these. After a few miles, shacks, a roadside market, stick-thin men pulling carts. Then it starts: urban *merde*, the bustees, wooden boxes topped with slate, with laundry and with what I took to be a sort of orange pasta, but which turned out to be cow patties. People washing at fire hydrants, modestly baring different sections of dark torso. More and more and more people thickening roadsides. Siren: nine o'clock. (We're an hour back of Rangoon time. I'm recovering the International Dateline Day.) Buses jammed. As we get close to Chowringhee, the buses are double-deckers. Thousands of stalls, shacks, people. Most of the last sit, stare, *perform* an intense sort of nothing. It smells less than I expected. (Perhaps Rangoon and Jakarta accustomed me to putrefaction.) Now and then, horrifying sights: pieces of animate gristle, people contorted like tables, chairs, sideboards. I remember Andy at nine wonder-

---

* I'd run into him in the Bangkok airport and again in Rangoon.

ing if chairs ever felt like getting up. A beggar comes to the jeep. His face is sticky with the horrible sweetness of the beggar boy in the Bogjoke [Rangoon] market. The city roads are gorged with carts, rickshaws, antique buses, antique cabs, antique cars. They drive in the middle of the road. Much horn blowing. My hotel is a three-sided, three-storied white affair with a lawn so perfect it could be used for tennis. The young, handsome man behind the desk appears to be English, but in response to my rude question says abruptly he's Indian: "Grandfather English." He has a handsome sister/wife/assistant, a more obviously Indian girl. One signs in a huge old register.

There's magnificence in Calcutta, it is not another Rangoon, eviscerated and spooky. There's stuff in the shops off Chowringhee, and across the way in the Maidan, shepherds, sheep, sheep-dogs, goats, cows. Street life: the "street people" with brass pots and the all-purpose shawl; begging boys are shooed away from me by old men.

Purchasing books: You tell a salesman you want "these books," he sends you to a man who gives you papers indicating that you want them, you take these to a cashier, and, after payment, give the receipt to the salesman, who carries the books to another man, who wraps them for you.

An editorial in the *Hindustani Times* about the difficulties of wearing saris in foreign slush.

Sign: "Commit no nuisance."

Night on the perfect lawn of the New Kenilworth: framed in the white stucco arms of the hotel are white metal lawn chairs in which people drink and snack on curried chicken. Across the street, workers hack at an eight-story building. (I ask the desk lady, "Is it going up or down?" This is not understood.) There's a lovely, spreading tree here, I don't know what kind, a few cats, and guards at the white iron gates. Little Russell Street is a quiet street, but only a few yards away from the hotel are six or seven street people. A father (or grandfather) rocks a two-year-old boy in his arms, murmuring something. What can it be? Is he telling him that the pot, the shawl, and the wooden box will one day be his?

I spend part of the afternoon getting my ticket to Katmandu straightened out. The Indian Airways people are nice to me, not to a saried lady arguing at the next desk. "I've missed two of my three appointments." "It is not my fault." "But it is." "No, madam. It is not my fault." She gets up, glares hatred, swishes off.

Glad I have to stay an extra day. Starting with defecation in the gutter and sight of the baby foot on the leg of the dark, homeless man, I begin to feel what Calcutta's about. First I rode to the Bijoli (to try and book a seat at Satyajit Ray's new picture). Endless noisy traffic. The raucous crunch suddenly stops: three cows stroll into the road. Paralysis; fury. They're off and we, to the marble Vishnu temple which I thought would be Mullish's palace on Rabindra Sarinan. The street is a human glacier. Every slow vehicle man has used clogs it: cart, hackney, jitney, samlor, rickshaw, trolley, bus, cab, oxen. It is lined with shops, stalls, hundreds of tiny commercial holes. There are hawkers, talkers, kibbutzers, messengers; and signs, specialists in undergarments and overgarments, boots and teeth, shoe laces and sexual dysfunction. And human beings in every possible shape, a man with a hand like a waiter's tray (bent the wrong way), a boy all stumps, a girl walking on her hands and feet like a dog and carrying a beggar's bowl in her teeth. Every kind of blotch, pustule, formation, and deformation.

A parade. "Communists," says the driver. Bursting in and out of Upper Chittaranji Street, fifteen hundred men in white, neat as the Rockettes, chanting, waving posters.

There is more life in five minutes of Upper Chittaranji Street than many people will ever see. It makes Bangkok klong life look bare as the Grand Canal in February. A human *pot-au-feu* of life. Tragedy, comedy, tragicomedy, spectacle, a billion annals, a million novels. A monument to human variety. Its icon is the statue of Gandhi on Chowringhee (now Nehru) Street. The stone man is alone, thin legs, staff and bald head as identifiable as the Don and Sancho in the park near the Madrid Ritz. As the Don and Sancho spell out the comic beauty of Spain, Gandhi radiates that fierce passivity which is the power of Hindu transcendence. India churns up its Gandhis of Not-me, the West churns up its billion Me's: spectators, victims, commentators, *mangiatori*.

Back at the hotel, four men work their way froglike across the lawn. What are they doing? Picking up uneven blades of grass.

Clouds

σὐράνιαι Νεφέλαι μεγάλαι Θεαὶ ἀνδράτιν ἀργοῖς
Clouds from heaven, perfect gods for idlers

ARISTOPHANES, Νεφέλαι *(Clouds)*

1

So many poems about clouds.
Still. Tonight (driving around
the mountains, inside a great
blue gap, there was a pack
of tiny, golden clouds: some were
letters: a *T*, an almost-epsilon,
an *O* (as if some smoke-ring puffer
had, just once, just made it).

My ancestors were message-hunters,
and though their alphabet is dark
to me, and I believe in next
to nothing they believed in, I
can use an unexpected message.
(There's been no mail out here at all.)
For seconds then, I pressed
that cirric alphabet like
a scholar with papyrus bits.

2

Now, against a ravishing
Tiepolo cloud, an almost straight
white line grows and grows.
A jet. Visible only in
its own debris. A straight white
line, as if the Scribbler

in Clouds decided to surprise
His readers with a human form.

But that's just it.
Like lines you make in manuscript
to signify italics, the jet
had sent its message: "Geometry
is here. Look sharp. Yours truly."

Inside Narcissus

*"Inside Narcissus" was written for a Princeton lecture in
1976 (I think). I remember rewriting it on that Tooner-
ville train from Princeton to Princeton Station. During the
talk, I revised en route. Few noticed. (Few were there.)
When I gave it next—at Johns Hopkins—I rewrote it
again. In the two years between its acceptance (by* Yale
Review*) and its appearance, much pertinent matter came
my way.* Yale Review *uses no footnotes, so the published
text looked like a belly pregnant with sextuplets. In any
event, the essay came out of and reflects exhaustion. (In
1976 I was worn down either by writing or suffering
Natural Shocks.)*

*The Narcissus portion of the essay is rooted in an old
enchantment with Horace Gregory's superb translation of
the* Metamorphoses. *I'd read a bit of the original in 1951
when I exchanged Latin for English lessons with a graduate student at the University of Frankfurt. I wasn't doing
too well, partly because of a cortical obtundity in the
linguistic section of the brain, partly because I was simultaneously exchanging English for Italian lessons with
a barber at the Frankfurt Military Exchange Post. The
point of the Italian was not only to read Dante but to get
a job in Rome. My tutor helped me write a long plea to
the Personnel Officer in Rome. I delivered this telephonic
monologue; it met with an incomprehensible response for
which the only Italian I could manage was, "I can't hear
you, the connection's poor." I did not call back. Which
ended not only a Roman career but my Italian and Latin
lessons. The Frankfurt assignment (teaching illiterate sol-*

*diers for Troop Information and Education) was over,
and we sailed home.*

*When I got my first full-time teaching job in 1954 (at
Connecticut College in New London), I taught a bit of
Ovid and translated lines 243–69 of book 10 of the
Metamorphoses for the class. Since the passage (and the
episode from which it's taken) embodies a theme of this
book, I print it here:*

Pygmalion, who had watched whores thrive,
Shrank from such vice and would not wive,
Carved, instead, out of some snowy stone,
A woman free from all defect and stain.
His statue seems to breathe, seems to desire,
As 'twere modesty alone restrained its fire.
So art hides art—and so Pygmalion loves
This semblance of life which almost lives.
Often his hand moves on his work to try
Whether its stuff be flesh or ivory,
Will not admit the last, but, with a kiss,
Kindles in stone, he thinks, responsive bliss.
He speaks to it, grasps it, seems to think
His fingers bruise where in the flesh they sink.
He courts it now with gifts and gallantries,
Smooth stone and speech, tears from the Heliades,
Shells, lilies, small birds, gems,
A necklace round its throat, silk on its limbs.
Adorned, it's beautiful, unadorned, the same.
He lays it on a couch on quilts of flame,
Rests its head on pillows soft as air,
He thinks it relishes the softness there.

A MODERN LIFE which is productive or peculiar is a kind of license to explain itself. And who isn't delighted by such explanation? Poets, politicians, muggers or musicians who won't supply their inside stories look as if they're trying to put something over on us. Magic is O.K. for kids, but the rest of us need truth; and not just the cover truths distributed to the naive, but the truths behind the truths.

Every fundamental particle appears to contain more fundamental ones, so every inside story has its story. In the Age of Openness, this story is what we require. For us, the hidden is sinister, perhaps criminal. (Real criminals serve up their careers along with all other self-sellers.)

The wonderful result is that we know more about thousands of remarkable people—a few remarkable because they've been remarked—than people in epochs of discretion knew about their neighbors, their kings, and, in a way, themselves.

For it is the case that knowledge of others promotes self-knowledge. It is a democratic and technological glory that millions of human beings are more sensitive to their specialness than all but the pharaohs and poets of darker ages. Democracy and mass media require a sense of individuality in their participants. A collective "you" is broadcast, but in reception it is singular. (Individuals, not collectives, buy detergents.) And technology has democratized the apparatus of commemoration: Instamatics harvest billions of smiles, tape recorders as many babbles. These fill parochial annals. Official files are stuffed with equivalent information. Pollsters sample opinions, archives store the whorls of a billion pinkies.

So scrupulously observed, sifted, recorded, who could resist caring for himself? Who could help becoming a narcissist?*

The literature of narcissism climbs every molehill of the inner landscape. No quirk too quirky, no wound too foul, no encounter too repellent for exhibition.

Old portraits were indicted for omitting warts; contemporary portraits are often rashes of them beneath which one tries to discern features. Want your portrait painted? Your biography written? Better come up with a new and better wart. (The odor of glue rises from quite a lot of innocent flesh.)

Honesty, frankness, authenticity, nothing up the sleeve. With our history, who can fault such mottoes? Abandon cover, ye who enter modernity. Right on.

Until the emperor of concealment [Richard Nixon] signed a bill which helped depose him, even the government subsidized self-exhibition in the form of tax write-offs for donated diaries, notebooks, letters, early drafts, the pencils which wrote them, the sharpeners which sharpened them.

The materials of self-revelation have altered not only conceptions of creation but creations themselves. They alter the lives of the creators as well.

More and more, makers and doers understand that part of their responsibility is to supply the "story of their story."[†] After all, better arrange your own show on a wide screen than have peephole versions of it sold in porn shops. Better donate to libraries than have your garbage sifted, bugs put in your martini olives.

---

* I don't employ—or discount—the psychoanalytic specificity, libidinal egoism.
† This was Henry James's phrase.

So makers and doers become their own specialists, their own voyeurs.

A few antique types believe art should conceal not only itself but the life behind it. Like James and Hardy, they burn papers; like Auden and Eliot, they forbid biographies; like Joyce, they warn wives to keep letters secret; like Shakespeare, they warn posterity off their bones. The results of such injunctions are well known. No one is more observed, more hungered after than the reluctant self-exhibitor. These creators are concealed somewhere in the bibliographical continents named after them.

A little while ago, I read an interview (in the *Chicago Daily News*) with one of these reluctant dodos, Philippe Petit, the funambulist who walked the air between the towers of the World Trade Center. He began the interview by remembering one given after that feat: "I was speechless when they asked me why I did it. Would you ask a kid why he climbed a tree?" No longer speechless—self-revelation is addictive—Petit went on to explain: "I did it because I like to climb. I like to feel fresh air and see the world from an unusual angle. I like to be alone and that's it." Even so decent a statement wasn't quite *it*. Petit came back to a position of security: "I think if we accepted more things without asking why, life would be a bit more interesting." Maybe, but even in Eden, half the human population didn't feel that way.

Petit is, however, on to something. Talking from the uneasy perch of the highwire performer, he senses the peril of abusing his insider's privileged position. The performer or creator may contain the inside story, but can he publicize it? Can he know it himself? If Petit were to analyze his motivations and muscle tensions while walking the highwire, it would likely be his last analysis. His very advantage would be his problem. (According to Ovid, Narcissus said, "Since I am what I long for, then my riches are so great, they make me poor.")

There is one sort of maker who is driven to narcissism by his occupation. This is the writer.

As athletes use their bodies, writers use their feelings, their insights, their fantasies, and, sometimes, the very events, the very shape and feel of their lives. Charged with revealing the world, the writer has learned that the world he reveals is conditioned by his way of observing it, and this by his feelings. (This last is not true of the physicist.) Many writers, therefore, have devoted themselves to self-examination and the exhibition of what Augustine called "the abysses of human consciousness."

Centuries before Augustine, Horace praised his satiric predecessor Lucilius for laying out his whole life "as if it were painted on a votive tablet." It was, though, not till the late sixteenth century that a writer claimed that he wrote because he knew nothing special but himself. Montaigne puzzled over his self-assignment. "Is it reasonable," he asked, "that I, so fond of privacy in actual life, should aspire to publicity in the knowledge of me?" He decided that this contradiction, like all others, was integral to his enterprise, which was revealing all of himself (*mon être universel*), or at least as much as decorum or caution allowed. "I speak the truth, not my fill of it, but as much as I dare speak."

"I want to know myself," Socrates told Phaedrus, a momentous conversion of the knower into the object of knowledge. "Knowledge cannot know the knower," goes an earlier text (from the Vedas), and many others describe obstacles to Socratic satisfaction. "I never can catch *myself* without a perception and can never observe anything but the perception," wrote Hume in his *Treatise on Human Nature*. Psychoanalysis describes hundreds of ways human beings hide from themselves.

How deal with such obstacles to observation of the interior? Physicists construct delicate enormities to register indirect effects; writers too have, over centuries, developed instruments of analysis and exhibition of the whirling interior. Varieties of lyric, hierarchies of illusion—plays within plays, tales within novels—soliloquies, letters, dramatic and interior monologues, fragmentation of narrative, passion-altered chronology, all are attempts to get hold of the flux.

Eighteenth-century fiction writers were as conscious of their instruments as twentieth-century ones of theirs. Richardson said of the letters in *Clarissa* that they "are written while the hearts of the writers must be supposed to be wholly engaged on their subject . . . so that they abound not only in critical situations, but with what may be called *instantaneous* descriptions and reflections." This technique was adopted, altered, parodied, and dropped until picked up again with variations (as, say, in *Wake Up, Stupid* or *Herzog*).

Fine books survive the techniques of presentation in the amber of literary perspective, the literary equivalent of the "museum without walls."

Interior analysis has a similar trajectory. We enjoy Clarissa and Lovelace though we know that much of what they think would not be thought by anyone we know. Interior analysis alters as it records ever-odder reactions to evermore minute and eccentric sensation and event. This doesn't mean that novels, memoirs, or human beings are improving. It means only that good novelists don't repeat their predecessors and also that people take stock of more and more peculiar reaction. Lovelace is a complicated fellow, but much simpler than Julien Sorel; Julien is crystal clear next to Stavrogin, and Stavrogin is but part of what the narrators of Proust or *Dr. Faustus* or *Humboldt's Gift* eat for breakfast.

Each large advance into the interior abyss makes the old charts obsolete, and usually it bewilders even the best readers. So fine a one as Erich Auerbach said of the complex fiction of his own time—which he brilliantly described—that there was "often something confusing, something hazy" about it. The works "leave the reader with an impression of hopelessness." Auerbach attributed the "hopelessness" to authorial sentiment, but to those who today read, say, *Ulysses* as a work of essentially serene comedy, the "hopelessness" belongs more to Auerbach's bewilderment at the new interior map than to the novel.

It is, I think, in part because the demand for analysis grew so much that fiction writers either bypassed it altogether or drew increasingly on their own experience. Despite the limits on self-knowledge, despite the dangers of self-exhibition, a writer at least felt confident about his feelings. If his memory were distorted, the distortion itself didn't betray fiction. If anything, it stood for strong feeling—which is what counts most. And narrative operation on such memory is likely to rouse more powerful feeling than treatment of less intimate material.

In any event, this justifies an excavation which often has serious personal consequences for the excavator and those he exhibits along with himself. It may be awareness of such consequences (as well as general disgust at any narcissistic display) which lies behind derogations of autobiographical writing. Montaigne complained about the complaints that he spoke too much about himself. Complaints today are more elaborate. Analytic literature—it's said—belongs to a class-ridden time of exclusive self-confidence in which bourgeois authors ignored their limitations and claimed omniscience. Modern fiction should—these critics say— be more modest, less direct. Like the sciences, it should reveal its apparatus with its findings.[‡] Program notes should accompany, even substitute for the old-time main event.[*]

Roland Barthes distinguishes between "writers," those who invent, and "those who write," that is, those who use the "prefabricated" material of their lives or the world. A case can be made that most literary matter is prefabricated—conventions of presentation, syntax, diction—but the Barthes distinction animates many a charge leveled at self-exhibition.

The antipersonal weapon which most affected my apprentice years was T. S. Eliot's famous injunction to be as disengaged from one's work as a chemical catalyst from the compound it catalyzed. Since young writers tend to go at the typewriter the way birds go at the air, making territorial claims of uniqueness with more or less tuneful bellyaching and brio, my writing pals and I were glad to turn ourselves into Sam Spades of the street, tailing our *données* to narrative connections, and dispatching them efficiently. Young Joyce didn't need more than a look at a priest's face—or a clock's—to take off; neither did we.[†]

[‡] Gide's *Les Faux-Monnayeurs* is a distinguished example of this peek-a-boo-with-your-mirror technique.

[*] Nathalie Sarraute's *Les fruits d'or* is an example of such substitution.

[†] Years after discarding the poet's chemical advice, it was still a bit of a shock to read that he hadn't been the literary dandy we'd thought. At least, of his most famous poem, he'd said that it was only "the relief of a personal and wholly insignificant grouse against life. . . . a piece of rhythmical grumbling."

The harshest critics of autobiographical fiction are often those who've just finished writing it. It's not so much "Why did I do it?" as "Thank God, that's over. Never again. I've had it. What relief. From now on, I'll write about the first thing that comes into my head."

Many writers do follow autobiographical works with very different ones, satires, travel books, utopian fictions, or short stories which seem merely hospitable to distant matter. At least, most of the writers I know tell themselves—or me—that this is what they're going to write. And they—we—may cover lots of pages about, say, the deaf janitor and his pet wolf. These pages seldom turn into books. They don't "sound right." The writer tries different "voices," different angles, different ways of telling the story. One day he hits on a way that seems to go. The book takes off and, a few years later, comes out. The writer gets the reviews and reads, "Here's another piece of Krumbacher's pretty carpet." Or, "Why doesn't old Krumbacher try something new?" It's the old Borges story of the artist who painted an immense landscape of brooks, mountains, and meadows which turned out to be a self-portrait.

Many fine fiction writers would be wiped out if they were prevented from using their own experience for their books. Isaac Babel told an interviewer, "I can't make anything up. I have to know everything down to the last wrinkle or I can't even begin to write." One of the splendors in Bellow's work is the suggestion that there's an infinite amount to say about his characters. They're like the pictures of Van Eyck in which you at least believe that if you took a magnifying glass to a tiny figure in some back-

---

Would Einstein claim that relativity theory was a piece of mathematical distemper? Was the Declaration of Independence only Jefferson's grouse about taxes on Monticello?

ground gathering, you'd be able to identify which king's head adorned the medallion on his coat. In Bellow's books there is the same sense of totality. The pages gleam with observations about the flesh, the voice, the eyelids, the odors, the gestures and expressions of the characters. Bellow told me that he needs real people in mind as a kind of sea from which to draw the endless detail which his narrative makes coherent.

A hundred years ago, Henry James reported to his brother William about Turgenev's dependence on actuality. Turgenev told him—said James—that "he had never invented anything or anyone. To his sense, all the interest, the beauty, the poetry, the strangeness etc. are there, in the people and things . . . in much larger measure than he can get them out and that (what strikes him himself as a limitation of his genius) touches that are too *raffiné*, words and phrases that are too striking, or too complete, inspire him with an instinctive *méfiance*; it seems to him that they can't be true—for to be true to a given individual type is the utmost he is able to strive for."

All right then, granted some fine writers claim they can't make anything up, that they have to draw every wrinkle from an actual face, that their creativity consists largely in the filtration of what strikes them as inconsistencies in actuality, still, why do some of these writers have to draw on their own intimate lives, on the people they know best, those whom they love? Why do they write about their own love affairs, children, divorces, the lives and deaths of their closest friends?

The fiction writer who wants his work to be a source of truth as well as diversion, beauty, merriment, whatever, may be unable to cut himself off from those situations which have affected him most deeply, and those situations may be impossible to detach from those who figured in them. It is sometimes next to impossible for a writer to shift even the locale of an event that gripped him. (Observe Henry James, in his *Notebooks* trying to get rid of Paris as the scene of Strether's advice to little Bilham.) The writer requires conviction before he can convince others. At least this is true of the writer who is not essentially a magician delighting in the tricks of his craft.

How then transfer a passion from the body which aroused it to a different one? How transform it from a love of person to, say, a love for money? It can be done, it has been and will often be done, but *sometimes* it is very difficult to do. The work is rooted in a pattern so compelling that to break it would be to break the back of the book. "I must know down to the last wrinkle." For some, that knowledge is bounded by what *has been*, what *is*.

Yet a Babel or a Turgenev must feel the joy of that work which has little to do with the xeroxing of events. Even if the source of the joy is absorption in the arrangement of a selected reality, it answers the fictional impulse to take off, to break out of quotidian schemes.

It's a truism that actuality is altered not only in memory but in the process of expressing it. What a Japanese tradition calls *muga*, "the removal of even a hair's breadth between the writer's will and his expression," is, I would guess, impossible. If a writer thinks he has written precisely what he wanted to write, my guess is that he's so pleased with what he reads, he thinks it's what he intended to say. Forster's famous remark that he couldn't know what he thought till he saw what he said is closer to the bull's-eye.

Such verbal transformation of experience is usually insufficient for either the fiction writer or the libel lawyer retained by his supposed models.

Story itself is discerned and felt very differently by the lawyer, historian, reporter, and the fiction writer. The first three must get things right in such a way that their reports can be checked out along the world's time and space schemes.

The fiction writer's story, even when it originates in actuality, comes to be dominated not by it as much as by the writer's feeling of coherence, amplitude, pace, his preferred ratio of scene to monologue, vertical—or sensuous—horizontal—or narrative—matter, his sense of comic or pathetic form, or what have you. And of course every alteration made to suit such preferences entails others. Reportorial omission deforms not just truth but the whole enterprise of reporting; fictional omission is intended to intensify and embellish; it is a requirement of most fiction.

All right, the fiction writer has gone down into the "rag-and-bone shop" of his heart for his story. There among the grievances, nutty ambitions, wild needs, fears, resentments, and manic plea-bargains he finds the rueful story of his wife's love affair with the mailman. He sets out to tell it, but, remembering when her hair seemed redder than it was, he makes her hair red, he fattens her lover and puts him in a different line of work, one which has always seemed a little sinister.

Shrink the tall, change the sex of the children, move them to Arizona, no, you've never been there and don't feel like taking a trip or making the place up out of old westerns, let's make it Wisconsin. The easiest thing to change is yourself. Make yourself better looking, no, uglier, and more naive, poorer; instead of your lisp, give yourself a bad leg and a profession rich in a technical vocabulary, which will suggest certain habits of mind or send you to places it'll excite you to work into the narrative. You know your own faults, let your character admit them, or better, save them for big scenes; let the wife, children, and the doctor friend lash him with them. (Didn't Dante do this beautifully in canto 30 of *Purgatory*? Beatrice is so hard on the Dante character that the angels try to intervene.) There is a kind of purgation in such indirect confession, a special pleasure in this indirect honesty. Put in that time you stole Billy's pen, but, well, let the ex-mailman get punished for it. (Didn't Proust say that Dostoevsky split the crime and punishment in his own life between two characters?)

All right, now you're home free to tell this thing the way it rolled over you, knocked you for a loop, putting you where you are now.

So the book gets written, version succeeding version, ideas pouring in from actuality or from delighted invention. *L'appetit vient en mangeant.*

Three years later, it's published. Friends poke you in the ribs: "You sure showed Charley." Your exwife tells you to stay away from the children. A learned ex-friend quotes Lord Hervey: "He never remembered an obligation nor forgot an injury."

It's not a total loss. The book's done, you've got a little money, you buy a Mercedes, send the kids to the shore, give your ex-wife the New York edition of Henry James; you enjoy some praise, work up froth at thimble-brained reviewers, float for a while, busy yourself with this and that, then start feeling for the next book.

But the tank's empty. You're worn out. Maybe you should take off and see something. The Serengeti, Kabul, Washington. There isn't a decent novel about American politics. No, we're politicked to death. How about the multinational world? The key institution of the late twentieth century. What a terrific mesh of interests. You read up, see characters forming out of Harold Geneen, Howard Page, African strong men.

No go. It sounds like bad Waugh.

You hole up in the country with Japanese novels, French memoirs, Dostoevsky, case histories of the broken, the assailed. You've never done a story about the dregs. Get out on Skid Row. Advertise for a rapist. Maybe a female rapist. Daughter of a multinational executive. An Emma with the soul of Smerdyakov.

You give it a try, but it doesn't go either. Nothing works. The trouble is your life. It's killing you. Lunch, dinner, the same talk. Everything veiled, evasion instead of drama. Granola instead of passion. You can't write *Karamazov* in a nine-to-five life. Get cracking. Take a chance. What about that girl who wrote you about your book?

The point is that the frequent messes, the complications in the lives of many writers are not unrelated to the business of making up stories. The contradiction between the feeling which generates the work and the necessary routine of the working life can, after working hours, lead to trouble. "Woe weeps out her division when she sings." If there's no woe, there may be no song. The writer knows that some of his finest passages have come after his heart has been rattled around and he's gone to a typewriter and put down more or less exactly what he's felt. He thinks he needs more rattling.

I write these lines shortly after I lay flat on a table while a camera swivelled over my chest and took centimetric pictures of one of my lungs. A jovial Hawaiian technician was hoping to find on these tomographs what had shown up indistinctly on cruder X-rays so he could go to lunch. He thought he'd found it, and, as his stomach bubbled, my heart sank. Yet, simultaneously, I was about the writer's business of noting his expression, the look of the machine, the coffin-size depression in the ceiling above it, and, above all, the shape of my own feelings, at least those I could separate from my writer's business. It was a diversion from the unpleasantness of ugly discovery. (Happily, the electronic Columbus didn't discover America.)

2

There is something ignoble about this process. Is one only a snooper? Is one's work so local an exercise? Will it be forgotten as soon as its little fibrillations of inside story and local color yield to the next wave of narcissistic snooping?

I think older artists often begin to think like this. The contradictions between life and work, between adherence to getting things exactly right and getting things said beautifully, between the desire for fidelity and the distortions of expression wear one down. Here is Conrad on the subject in the remarkable preface to *A Personal Record*:

> I have always suspected in the effort to bring into play the extremities of emotions the debasing touch of insincerity. In order to move others deeply we must deliberately allow ourselves to be carried away beyond the bounds of our normal sensibility—innocently enough, perhaps, and of necessity, like an actor who raises his voice on the stage above the pitch of natural conversation—but still we have to do that. . . .
>
> . . . the danger lies in the writer becoming the victim of his own exaggeration, losing the exact notion of sincerity, and in the end coming to despise truth itself as something too cold, too blunt for his purpose—as, in fact, not good enough for his insistent emotion.

Genuine as it may be, Conrad's doubt seems to me related to a discouragement with one's art which writers often experience in their last years. Rare is the writer who writes to his dying day with undiminished belief in his art. Perhaps the greatest of such authors, Proust, said a few days before his death that his work contained nothing but his "deep and authentic impressions" which flowed from "the natural progress of [his] thought." That is the rarest sort of declaration. (Even it is conditioned. Anyone who's seen Proust's manuscripts knows that "natural progress" was closer to the tumultuous trial-and-error of natural selection than to, say, Niagara Falls.)

Narrative may be the deepest of humanizing patterns, one which begins in what René Spitz calls the "primal dialogue" between mother and child. All we know and feel is evaluated in terms of this deep story which is oneself. More than theory, it determines what we observe and how we feel about it. It shapes the way we love and even the way we die.

Yet narrative art is the least sensuous of the arts. Its material is essentially impalpable, invisible, silent and motionless. The codified scribbles (or unmusical phonemes) suggest all other senses, but only suggest them. Narrative compensates for this dryness in the fluency and suggestibility which give it a hammerlock on memory. Its ability to slide up and down in time as well as in and out of the human interior makes it the art to which almost no one is totally deaf. But that dryness, that abstract matter, gives the older writer little support. Old painters muck about with paint, old musicians have keys to hit, sounds to keep them afloat. The writer isn't nourished by the physical matter of his art, and this reinforces the contrast between the assurance and tranquility indispensable to creation and the turbulence which is so much of narrative subject matter. That immateriality of narrative, so perfectly suited to fluid retrospection, puts next to no physical barrier between the writer and his work. It is another invitation to narcissism; and like others we've described, it promotes Conradian bafflement. What counts most, the mysterious exaltation of what is ultimately self-transcending or, at least, self-transforming work, is, in time, ground down by these peculiar conditions. The contrast between the deeply felt beauty of the art and the deeply troubling jaggedness of the life which generates it becomes insupportable. The writer may say to himself what a brother narcissist, Muhammed Ali, said near the end of his third fight with Joe Frazier: "What am I doing here? I don't need to be doing this."

Stratford beckons. "I'll bury my book." Or, as one of Shakespeare's favorite authors, the self-exhibiting Montaigne, put it: "Any man can play his part in the sideshow and represent a worthy man on the stage; but to be disciplined within, in his own bosom, where all is permitted, where all is concealed—that is the point. To be disciplined in our actions where we don't have to account to anyone, where nothing is studied or artful, that is the next step."

Prose-Thumbing

Oh, the loathsome egocentricity of these experimentalists.

1. No beginning.

2. *Dans ma rêve*
   Il y a une grève.

3. In my dreams
   There is a strike. (Or 'beach'?)

4. In my heart
   Squats a tart,

5. Learning Spanish.
   En mi cabeza
   Está un . . . bezo.

   In my head, there is a wound.

   Off-rhyme.

Try *cabezo*: *Summit of hill* or *mountain*; *reef*; *shirt-collar*; *falling-band*. What does Señor Cuyás (of *Appleton's New Spanish-English and English-Spanish Dictionary*, 1920) mean by the last? (Is the good Cuyás a secret poet? A subversive lexicographer?)

On my summit
There's a wound.

Not bad.

(On my summit, there is vummit. *Pas très fort.*)

En mi corazón
no está razón.

from my heart

reason doth part.

Hasta luego, poet.

6. Translation's for the *uccelli*. One tongue at a time. Though consider the honorable perspiration of S. Beckett of the Rue Saint-Jacques. Does his French; then his English; and the reverse. However, the *corazón* of this fine gentleman's constructions is constriction. As for Nabokov, V., Joyce, J., and Infante-Cabrera, G., they either straw-boss teams of the intimidated or mess themselves. (Evidence: the four volumes of N's *Eugene Onegin*; the Engleesh junk of *Tres tristes tigres*.) No evidence-here-of the practice of such bilinguals as S. Merrill, J. Green, or J. Korzenowski Conrad.

7. Herr Dr. T. Mann told me (Bad Gastein, August 1951) that he learned English reading Mrs. Lowe-Porter's translations of his work. (I tried with *Las hijas de los otros*, [Buenos Aires: Editorial Sudamericana, 1975]. Was bored. Why chew old gum?)

8. a) I borrow this numerical organization from L. Wittgenstein (who did not originate it).
b) A man after some of my *corazón* (if I can trust the fine portrait in N. Malcom's memoir. Is it a true picture of that human proposition?)

9. Automatic writing. Of sorts. Not à la G. Stein in lab of W. James. Nor John Donne, distracted in prayer by flies, describing the distraction. Nor the-transcribed-dying monologues of John Brown and Dutch Schultz. Nor Mr. Burroughs's prescription: write only what your senses dictate. (Or something to that labile in-effect.) Mine issued by the Imp of the Machine. The *machine à écrire. Le Diablotin de la Littérature.* Cere-

bral motion; accompanying hand's. (Hand—said Lawrence, D. H.—as much *me* as brain.)

10. Nothing to brain here. (Little to hand.)

11. Mudlaw's face: razory pink, theoretical eyes: blue, theory-full mouth. Cheerily drear. Conversation-maker. And keeper. Frankly mendacious.

12. Two days ago, my birthday; two days from now, off to Guatemala; Bogotá; Brazil. L. Wittgenstein adored the films of the banana-hatted "Brazilian bombshell" Carmen Miranda. And Betty Hutton. 's films. The stars that shine in starry heads. Witt., exhausted by two philosophizing hours went daily to the flicks. (His word.) The worse the better. Totally absorbed—says Malcolm—in them. W. gave away his fortune. First endowed—anonymously—Rilke and Trakl. Schoolmaster, soldier, architect, musician, sculptor. Behind all the "new" philosophy which calls all in—linguistic—doubt. Chomsky's underwriter. A depressive. Last words: "Tell them I've lived a wonderful life."

13. What would the thirteenth commandment have been?

14. "Thou should not wipe thy heinie with thy shirt."

15. "*Du sollst nicht dein Poopoo mit dein Hemd abwischen.*"

16. A language cretin, I'm always languaging. T. Mann accused—circa 1948—of writing in English, said—in Bad Gastein, August 1951—"My country is *deutsch*." "*Mein Vaterland ist German.*" ('tis of thee)

17. In my dream there is a wish
    And a memory of fish.

18. W. H. Auden

19. T. Mann's son-in-law. (So that Erica Mann could get out of Germanland.)

20. For getting her out . . . forgetting.

21. Auden's face. Sinclair Lewis's face. Pits, trenches, welts, hillocks. Auden (Chicago, 1966 or '67): "Three bad men who were good poets, Yeats, Brecht and—was it?—"Claudel."

22. They abused women. (Did Claudel? I think not.) I think that was Auden's reason. (For not getting women out. For remembering them.) More to it than that.

23. There is always more to it.

24. I am not an experimental writer. This story is off (my) limits. It is not a story. Prose? On the whole.

25. Whatever it is, take it.

26. Or don't.

27. The author is twenty-one years old.

28. I have just made it a work of fiction.

29. Truly yours,

30. *Richard Stern*

The book's title essay is in part about itself. (Self-explanatory.) A word though about the "self," the "I" that runs through it. It's a more naive "I" than is found in most of this book. It's the "I" of college lecturing. (And the formality and naiveté hint at the danger of a long teaching career. One must keep interrogating not only one's word and deeds but one's thoughts, which are habitually nastier, at least rowdier, and so closer to what counts for one's work.) Despite these cautions of "soft shoulders on the road," I keep the essay as a rough map of the country.

The Invention of the Real

"Real" is not a normal word at all . . . but highly exceptional; exceptional in this respect that, unlike "yellow" or "horse" or "walk," it does not have one single, specifiable, always-the-same meaning."

J. L. AUSTIN, *Sense and Sensibilia*

"Margaret," said Marianne, with great warmth, "you know that all this is an invention of your own, and that there is no such person in existence."

"Well, then, he is likely dead, Marianne, for I am sure there was such a man once, and his name begins with an F."

JANE AUSTEN, *Sense and Sensibility*

IMAGINE that you wake up the first day of your conscious life on some planet's moon. A space ship has somehow nourished and now abandons you. You have consciousness, a dozen years or so, a body. Nothing else but food and pills and bright lunar emptiness. There are no words in your world, no other beings at whom to grunt in wonder, terror, hunger.

Now imagine the stages of discrimination, but not with the sophisticated naïveté of René Descartes. He was equipped with whole vocabularies of discrimination. But you, alone on that moon, are not even a complete "I"—for to be fully "I" there must be a sense of "you," of "it." Nor is the fuzz of glare and black, the flash-and-chill-charged kinesthesia exactly *thinking*. You *are*; you feel, see, puzzle, but can you make the assertion that you *think, therefore you are*? (Working out that *therefore* would require a combination of Einstein and Shakespeare.) Can you in fact make any assertion? Maybe, one day, shivering with chill as you approach the dark side of your moon, the noise of shivering on your lips becomes, as it were, the word for *cold*, and a light bursts inside your head with the pleasure of this naming. And maybe then you can begin assigning other varieties of moan and groan to walking, waking, swallowing pills, to bright, to dark, perhaps even to their orderly succession.

Would you ever attain to something that could be called an explanation of yourself? Your existence on this stone crust? Would you, that is, have what human beings need almost as much as they need air and water, the story of themselves: What am I? Who am I? (Of course on a one-person planet, "who" would be superfluous. So would many crucial human questions: What are others? Are they for me? Against me? Though a genius might conjure up: What is knowing and what can I know? What is happening to me? What does happening mean? How do I connect with this, separate from that? Am I the same awake as I was asleep? Awake today the same who awoke yesterday?

And: What is it all about? What is the meaning of these waking-sleepings, eating-emptyings, these easings, these distresses?)

Very early, surely, in the process of the humanization of humanoid creatures, story must have come in. Not just that separation of inner and outer which is perception and which naming transforms into cognition, but a coherent serialization of events which fuses process and personality. Is there anything else more humanizing? Is it even possible to say that this "storification" is itself the means of humanization?

I'm neither philosopher, psychologist, historian nor anthropologist. I sneak into a great university through a cellar window reserved for a class of falsifiers permitted that entrée as jesters were given privilege by old kings, for diversion, sometimes bitter, sometimes sweet. The fiction maker is even freer than the jester. His stories need never be checked against the time-and-space coordinates of those other reality-stories which order and dominate human life. He does have complicated social functions, but that isn't the business of this essay. This business has to do with the process itself—with invention. Not precisely with the invention of those special stories called fictions, but with a small portion of the story-making process as it occurred in me about a year ago.

I'd better qualify this. To some degree I want to describe a kind of essay or lecture-making process: that is, I will try to reproduce some of what I noticed last year from the story maker's viewpoint, a viewpoint that was conditioned by the title of this talk, one which I'd given in answer to a request a few days before I left on the trip. The conclusions, then, are reflections on the theme sounded when—

under pressure to come up with a title—I uttered the five words which I discovered on bulletin boards when I returned.

Its first dateline is one of the greatest of all story towns, Venice; the second is a small town visited on impulse; and the third is another of the four or five greatest of all story towns, Paris, where I report two conversations, one with a gentlemanly hoodlum, the second with another—rather more distinguished—story writer.

So to Venice.

1. Early September. This room is five feet above a canal. Moon and lamplight stipple the water. Two A.M., quiet as a deaf man's skull. The *fondamenta*—a street on a canal— is banked by three- and four-story houses, none eminent or especially handsome, but spookily beautiful now. Two bridges staple the gold-touched water. The room is filled with drawings, watercolors, pieces of sculpture. One of these, fixed to the wall, is a crucifix made by extending the outer tines of a fork. Joan—my hostess—says it was made by Ibrahim, a half-Jewish, half-Shiite Iraqi who shuttles between Paris and the Middle East, selling his work, looking for his children, and perhaps for an old dream of greatness which his shuttling life has dissipated.

I often wake to the warning cries of boatmen who steer garbage sacks or lovers around the bend of this canal. Then upstairs for coffee and rolls in Joan's workroom. She's carving a horse's head in black wax. It and her feisty dog, Sammy, make up the breakfast foursome. Two of us exchange juicy items from the local newspaper, the *Gazzetino*, which this morning reports that a woman in Lima, Peru, had her gold fillings stolen as she was riding a bus. "The thief," she explains to the police, "took advantage of me while I was yawning." The phone rings. A woman says (in Oxbridge English): "Hello. This is the Queen of ————" and names a country that has for thirty-odd years been ruled by a well-known dictator. I repress the impulse to say, "And how is King ———— [the name of the dictator]?" because I know that this lady is no crank, but was, once upon a time, the official queen of that country, and that her father, king of a neighboring country, died of his pet monkey's bite five months before her birth. I know too that she is now known in Venice for swiping rolls of toilet paper from the bathrooms of hotels which used to allow her to stay free of charge. Thirty-odd years ago, she was married to her little king—like herself, one of the numerous great-grandchildren of Queen Victoria—after a bitter political fight with her husband's mother. Once upon that time, she was a slender princess, raised for the strange life of royalty.* Now she's a twisted morsel of regal superfluity (a kind of Ibrahim's fork), yet part of some of the bloodiest episodes of twentieth-century history. The Queen announces she'll be by for lunch, that we shouldn't bother with champagne, she will content herself with fresh vegetables—preferably *fagiolini*—boiled and served *senza burro, senz'olio*.

I get in a *traghetto* and walk to Campo San Barnaba, where I buy a *cappuchino* and write in a notebook. Construction workers take an *espresso*-and-*grappa* break at a stand-up bar, but otherwise it's quiet in the little campo. Two of the other five people at the café are engaged on business similar to mine; a bald man, thirtyish, Austrian or German, writes fiercely in a school notebook; a young woman with glitter-rimmed eyeglasses sketches the church which gives the *campo* its name. At the store where I used

---

*This is described in a heart-rending and bathetic book which, though ghost-written, is a self-exposure almost beyond decency.

to buy books when I taught here in 1962–63, there is a sale, and I've picked up a volume of poems by one Alfonso Gatto, born in 1909. I read a four-liner called "Giotto":

Nulla che non sia dolce e buono
e l'uomo e la montagna uguali
e la casa come la mano
posato per questa sera

Not bad, I think, just the thing for my lecture. I write a translation in my notebook:

Nothing which isn't good and gentle
the man and the mountain equal
and the house, like the hand
posed for the evening

The girl sketching, Joan and Ibrahim will understand this. In the artist's hierarchy, mountain, man, house, and hand lose their worldly priority and are—in the evening painted by Giotto—just different-colored shapes.

Back at Joan's. The doorbell rings. It's not our sad queen, but a scrawny ancient, magnificently dressed in a striped, rust-colored turban and matching ankle-length dress. "I yam," she says in a Russian-phonemed English, "ovairrrcome." It is Madame—I will call her—Incognita who dressed the world's rich and famous in the thirties and forties. Her husband fell in love with Greta Garbo, and, rumor goes, so did Incognita. Today, decades later, she and Garbo, though they live in the same New York apartment house, do not speak to each other. Now Incognita is distraught. Her "vairry bast friend," Count (I'll call him) Sigismundo, died yesterday afternoon at the "vairry moment when I am buying pitches in the *campo*" She is, she says, "feenished with Eetaly, feenished with Vainice." Sigismundo, she says, was the last representative of "high style" in the city. "Canal Grande feenish. All is feelth and chipness." She offers her historical analysis: "Eet begeens with feelthy jins"—blue jeans—"than comes knifes." That is, the terrorists of Italy's Red Brigade are the inevitable consequence of wearing blue jeans. After that comes "Ravolushon wheech I saw, nine years olt, weeth mine own eyes in Sebastopol."

The Count's funeral will be Friday. "The thirteenth?" asks Joan. Incognita's still beautiful eyes grow huge in blue fright. "Friday ze *four*-teens! Ze sirteens I do not leaf my rrooom. Ze sirteens *I stay hum*."

Two days later, we go to the funeral service in the nuttily baroque church of San Moise.[†] The church is usually empty, the priest is a famous bore, but today it is full of Venetian cream which the preacher, delirious with rapture at the crowd, churns into great curds of tedium. Finally, rhetoric subsides, the hat is passed, and we go into the *campo* to watch the mourners. The Countess, who has a face as sharp as the teeth on a gondola's prow, goes from group to group extending her wicked face for kisses. From the family Vendramin, she is usually called Contessa Benzadrine. She was an enthusiastic Fascist. In 1945 the partisans shaved her bald, stripped her naked, and ran her through the streets from the Stazione to the Piazza San Marco. Now she steps into the black funeral gondola which will take her husband's coffin to San Michele, the cemetery island.

I've touched here on a fraction of the people I saw in Venice last year, but you can see how even these flakes of

[†] Where the perpetrator of the first great stock swindle, John Law, is buried.

the reality-cake make promising story matter. Stories flow from any town—or from a hermit's cave—but story machinery has been pumping so long in Venice, that people feel licensed to act in provocative ways. And of course, the peculiarities of a carless, trainless, water city create such odd versions of human situations that there is theater on every street and *campo*. Then too, strangeness attracts the strange. So ex-queens come here, along with the idle, the decadent, the beautiful, the famous and would-be famous, most with time to make mischief, trouble, and stories. So much is this a story town that it's an obstacle to writing about Venice. How do you say anything new about a town where you can use a four-hundred-year-old map to get around?

The sort of permanence this suggests is the sort Alfonso Gatto drew on for his little poem on Giotto. The hands, the evening, and probably the houses Giotto painted are gone; their reality exists only in his painting; and we know it only as he did seven hundred years ago. (As for Gatto's twenty-five or thirty words, they too hold us for a minute or so, gattoize us as Giotto giottoized us.)

Even now, something like this is happening. A small part of me is becoming a smaller part of you, and for these moments, anyway, we are both somewhat altered, courtesy of a thirteenth-century painter, a modern poet, an ex-queen, and an eighty-year-old lady whom I have simplified into caricature.

2. A week later. I'm in Dôle, a small town on the Doubs River in the Jura. The town is best known as the birthplace of Louis Pasteur, whose house is sixty or seventy yards down the street where I write this. The house is darkened by a large sixteenth-century church on the hill above. Its

darkness reminds me of the especially dark darkness of Thomas Edison's house in the little town of Milan, Ohio. (When I saw it last year, it occurred to me that the inventor who transformed the nights of the world must have been especially conscious of the old helplessness of human nights.) Pasteur's town suggests an analogy with my subject, the storification of the real. The analogy comes to me at the table in the dining room of my little hotel, the Pomme d'Or.

Three hours ago, I was heading for Dijon, a gastronomic Jerusalem for Crusaders of the Belly. But the train stopped a few extra minutes at Dôle, and I (mistaking it for another town I'd enjoyed seeing and eating in several years ago) got off. It's turned out to be a sad little place, but one which conceals—at least contains—here, an (as far as I know) unsung artist who converts trout, bean, potato, and other earthly goods into culinary marvels. These direct me to my analogy.

Men and beasts share the chemical/mental complex called hunger and erase it with whatever they recognize as food. The recognition is infinitely more complex in men than beasts; so the jellied roaches which delight the gourmets of Osaka do different things to the hungriest Westerner. Already the basic reality, hunger, has been rerouted over a complex map. If we compare a tiger's devastation of a gazelle's ribs with the average Westerner's restrained arrangement of his appetite into breakfast, lunch, and dinner, or his conversion of a meal into occasions of reunion, domesticity, thanksgiving, intellectual exchange (à la Plato's *Symposium*), or religious communion, we see how that basic reality, hunger/food, is only a plank in the architecture of human consumption.

So stories convert the data of event into a coherence which doesn't just transform actuality, but creates it. That is, it makes sense out of sensation. Consciousness depends on storied notions. We say of a described character, "Ah. That's the way I feel. That's what I want to do." We alter by inventing new stories about ourselves and others. Between the—let's call it—biology which brings X to Y, and the decision to "go with" (let alone "marry"), falls story. "Is X the sort of person I want to spend a week with? A lifetime with?"

We're all story makers, constant inventors of the realities we call *our life*. Story-making pressure is so great, it continues in that nightlife of dreams in the direction of unresolved, that is *unstoried* tensions, fears, hopes, desires, hatreds, uncatalogued sensation.

October 1979 addendum: A recent American visitor displayed the power of story. A gray-haired man in a white dress went through the streets transfiguring the energy of millions of people. The pope, no different physically from a bench-sitter tossing nuts to a pigeon, is nonetheless a kind of human Venice, a package of stories. So he became part of millions of American story-makers.

3. This essay of three cities continues in Paris. I arrived September 19, thirty years to the day after my first arrival. I'm saturated with nostalgia, real and phony. I walk the street where a girl I was to marry lived and cross the bridge where I got the idea for the first story for which I was ever paid. Melancholy rapture takes over: "So much not done, so much gone wrong." An orgy of self-punishment, controlled by a little fund of self-satisfaction.

Two days later, reading *Le Monde* over a beer at the Café de la Marie, I find myself interrogated by a large-

bellied gentleman in an old tweed jacket and orange turtleneck, the top of which looks like a neck brace. I've noticed him because he's used his cane to open the door for a
spaniel whose master sits at a corner table. The old fellow
croaks, "*Sont-ils indiens?*" "They" are a young Vietnamese
woman and her small son. They've come in with an armful
of packages and sat down on my right. They speak English,
although the woman orders ice cream in good French. I tell
him the woman seems part Vietnamese, part French, the
boy American. I have overheard them saying they were
going back to Dallas. The man says I needn't whisper, then
invites me to consider history, in particular the history of
Rome (pronounced "Rrum"). Was I aware that that community was brought low by mongrels: "*les barbares*"? I
tell him I understand his point. Well then, I should look
about me. I should regard the menacing presence of the
Portuguese in Paris. Then there was Washington, D.C. Was
I aware of the enormous percentage there of *negres*? He
touches my newspaper. And what are we doing about this
ebony swine, Bokassa, so-called emperor of Central Africa? "The government has been cuddling this mongrel for
years. Now we're reduced to forbidding him landing rights
at Orly and Bordeaux. In my time," he says as if from the
grave, "we'd have sent in a battalion of paratroopers. Now
we can't afford to send in a gendarme with a revolver. All
our money went into the swine's coronation."

Well, this is certainly better than *Le Monde*. It's been a
while since I've encountered views like this in the flesh. I
pass my time in precincts where tolerance and enlightenment are scarcely violated in jokes. So I encourage the swin-
ish historian, offer him a cigar, nod as his insights open
tunnels in my ignorance, and supply only those responses
which will keep his golden spigot open. Twenty minutes

later, I've had it. "*Au 'voir, m'sieu.* It's been a great pleasure." Here I notice the spaniel's master regarding me with loathing. It's clear he sees me as cosponsor of my neighbor's repulsive views. Doesn't he know I'm only a literary provocateur, that this is research?

The next day I drink coffee at another café with another gentleman. I don't know him well—this is our second meeting in two years—but I like and respect him enormously. He is one of the few writers who's invented a type of person and experience so different from others that his name and theirs have become labels.

He too is somewhat melancholy. "I hate nine-tenths of everything I've written," he tells me. He has none of Madame Incognita's theatrical pessimism. He is personal, but not egotistic. She was comical, farcical; he is humorous and affecting. "I'm ashamed of my life," he says quietly. "The world's so full of misery. And what have I done? Words." Despite a surge of fellow feeling, I think of Hamlet's "And like a whore unpack my heart with words." But of course that unpacking is just one thing you do with words, and the creator of Godot, Lucky, Pozzo, Hamm, Malone, Murphy, Winnie, and Watt has not only unpacked his own but millions of hearts. He tells me his fiction came out of the dark. "I never had a plan for it. Never knew where it was going." His plays were written for relief. "They were all out there, in the light. Much easier. But the call comes from the dark." Now he'll write but not publish. "Just finishing translating a ten-thousand-word piece I wrote in English. I call it *Company.* Because I wrote it to keep myself company. Then I found the company even worse than my own." [‡] The words of the constant story

[‡] He changed his mind. *Company* is published.

maker keep coming: despite the misery out there, the—what?—energy within gets to the page, and the septuagenarian inventor of the Beckett world continues making it.

Like any manufacturer, an artist creates not only to satisfy a want—his own, his patron's—but to create wanters whom only he can satisfy. (Even if he is his own chief wanter.) Can we separate the producer from the product?

A nonpublishing Beckett will still be Beckett, but will a nonwriting Beckett? (If there is no web, shall we call the bug a spider?)*

Or is this the wrong question? There is the *Iliad*-Homer and his older self or careful successor, the *Odyssey*-Homer. There is the *Watt*-Beckett and the *Godot*-Beckett. What counts are *Watt* and the *Iliad*. Without them, or rather, without their successors, the invention of the real would stop and human beings would, each year, become less human.

---

* Yeats's poem wonders about telling "the dancer from the dance." How about an ex-dancer? Well, that's what he is then, an ex-dancer.

Who Knows?**

1.
Learning the postures of love, its peculiar measures,
there is no need to stumble, innocent
as Ali Baba at the cavern of pleasures.

When we were ignorant with infant wonderment,
continually desiring the same, incapable of sum,
it seemed the past itself was renascent;

But sprung from the tunnel, we gaped deaf and dumb
before the endless tracks, the railroad palace,
where one could lounge and drink and thumb

The schedules of malice,
laugh with antique wisdom
about old tours of phallus.

In the train, the wheels' kingdom,
we sat relaxed and taxed with sureness;
only Outside Error could corrupt The Boredom.

Our stomachs knew no qualms of nearness,
we were always *there* to laugh at
gauche intrusions of newness.

**I wrote "Who Knows?" in 1947. It belongs here as the nineteen-year-old's version of the nostalgia felt by the fifty-one-year-old of "The Invention of the Real."

2.

Some have known. For instance, Kafka
saw the flawless groundwork bloom
impossible bulbs, cough up

Monsters of unlikelihood, assume
invisible disguises. Trains delayed
false arrests made, love undermined.

These the enzymes that decayed
the sugars of his life and laid
him youthful in the ground, amazed, decayed.

This is the introduction to a talk given on March 14,
1979, USA Day—and the centenary of Albert Einstein's
birth—at the International Book Fair in Buenos Aires.
The talk began by recalling my only glimpse of the great
man. Age eight or nine, I was playing soccer in Central
Park, looked up to see the man with the—then—amazing
head of gray hair. I missed a ball which didn't miss me. It
ricocheted off my head, hit the bulb of a park lamp. The
bulb fell on my wool-capped head, and for seconds I was
out. I attributed my subsequent career as dreamer-writer
to the combination of astonishment and brain damage.

Orpheus at the Blackboard

Will you forgive the misshapen sounds if I begin with some
lines in Spanish?

> Es un error creer que las estrellas
> Puedan servir para curar el cáncer
> El astrólogo dice la verdad
> Pero en este respecto se equivoca.
>
> (PARRA, "Discurso Funebre")

> It's a mistake to believe
> That stars can cure cancer
> The astrologer tells the truth
> Though not in this respect.

Can one tell from these lines that the author is a professor
of theoretical physics?
Or that the lines

Los comuneros llevan la mañana
enredada en los dientes de sus hoces

(JORGE CARRERA ANDRADE, "Indiada")

The villagers left the morning
caught in the teeth of their sickles

are by an ambassador, a president of his country?

Or, if I can return with relief to my own language, that
the following lines are written by an actor clearly ashamed
of his work, at least of the fact that it makes him exhibit
himself in public:

Thence comes it that my name receives a brand,
And almost thence my nature is subdu'd
To what it works in, like the dyer's hand.

(Sonnet 111)

These lines are by that great Marxist writer, William Shakespeare. "My nature is subdued to what it works in, like the
dyer's hand." This is—in a way—the theme I've been given,
the theme of this conference. To what degree is the literature of this time altered by, affected by the fact that so
many of its authors make their living as professors in universities? I am Shakespearean, if not Marxist enough to
say that there are surely important consequences of this
fact. Marx himself was not so unsubtle a Marxist as to
maintain that a profession determined a human in his en-
tirety. At least, this was not the case for men and women
who made literature. For it is literature which is their profession, no matter how they find money to pay the butcher,
the baker, and the landlord. And literature signifies the
subtlest registration of personality. If there is such a thing
as individuality—what makes one human being differ from

another—it is expressed, if not created in literature, in those thousands of silent choices made by the writer at his typewriter. Literature, the art which depends least on performance, the least sensuous and public of the arts, the one which bursts into flames in that physical stillness in which a mind shapes a story, lives and dies by individuality. It has nothing else. For otherwise it is just the same thing by which we order our *parrillada* or tell each other where we've been. In these still moments, one is not physicist, diplomat, doctor, lawyer, beggar, or thief. One is mind. One mind discharges its intensely meditated, intensely labored delight in the verbal ordering of imaginary events to another mind which yields to it with the pristine curiosity of an amorous virgin.

Well, I seem to have destroyed the topic. I'm saying it ultimately doesn't matter whether writers make their living as university professors or pickpockets. This might be totally true if we were speaking of a purer order of men. Can you imagine a pickpocket with sufficient ease of mind to sit down and write a poem or story? But it's clear that writing poems and stories requires a certain peace of mind, a space of time. Some professions make it easier to write than others. And every worldly circumstance affects the writer's mind.

When I write, I write in a language; that is, I use words each so heavy with use that it is almost a miracle that any foreigner can feel their significance. Of course, you may carry this suggestion to unreal limits. I remember when the great Beethoven pianist Artur Schnabel said only German pianists could play Beethoven. In that case, only people from Bonn or Vienna could play him. Or further, only people who lived in Beethoven's house, or members of his family. Finally, only Beethoven himself could play and listen to

Beethoven. With that, the whole meaning of Beethoven's work dissolves. Human culture and society dissolve.

The idea of this Book Fair is to reinforce what counts so much, the expansion of the individual by the absorption of the new. The dissolution of foreignness. So every Spanish sentence I read makes me more Spanish, every Argentinian work I read in either fine English translation or, with the help of dictionary and friends, in Spanish, makes me partly Argentinian.

It is important that a writer writes in one language rather than another, and it can be important for some writers that they have grown up in New York and have passed most of their writing life in Chicago, as I have. Or, to cite a much more splendid writer, that your own Borges spent early years in Geneva and Paris before settling in Buenos Aires.

In another way, I am like Borges, and like so many other writers of this century. I have earned at least a part of my living lecturing university students. Of the hundreds of good writers in the United States, there are very few who do not make the most important part of their living teaching in universities. It is the dominant literary profession of the twentieth century, as the church was the dominant profession of the English poets of the first part of the seventeenth century, as the publishing industry was the dominant profession of the writers of the eighteenth century. In Latin America, many marvelous writers have made a living working in diplomatic posts for their countries.*

In the United States, literature has had a less conspicuous public role. At the recent dinner our president gave for the Chinese vice-premier, the only American writer

---

* I did not need to remind the audience of the Latin American writers who live in political exile.

there was a journalist who'd written a book about China. The vice-premier remarked that art and literature were the universals that bound men. Our good president (or his staff) may have felt that dragging such universal-makers out of their studies and bringing them to dinner hundreds and thousands of miles away would be doing them wrong. Perhaps. (And perhaps that's the reason there is no American novel comparable to Asturias's *El señor presidente* or Garcia Marquez's *The Autumn of a Patriarch*.)

Am I implying that the subject matter of the writer-teachers of my country is limited to university life? No, I'm not. Though it is clear that if it were possible to make a living working for years in the diplomatic service of the United States, as, say, St. John Perse and Paul Claudel worked for France or Pablo Neruda for Chile, and if one were, say, a novelist rather than a poet, there is a good chance that at least the subject matter of a novel or two would have to do with public power. But who knows. Does part 2 of *Faust* reveal the expertise of the great minister of the little state of Weimar? And has Marquez ever been a diplomat? Not as far as I know.

Q-and-A

*The interview is not a highly regarded genre. This special
fusion of drama, commentary and conversation is lower
in the mystic hierarchy of value than the essay or the
work of reportage.* Interviewing, like driving, brings out
bad stuff in us, desire to aggrandize, dominate, destroy. A
good interviewer is a person of value. The first interviewers here are particularly valuable to me because they
are friends and former students. The old relationship
helps inform the interview, which is richer for it. Jim
Schiffer, a brilliant writer and scholar, wrote an introduction in which I become one of his comic characters. Although it is the only direct description of me in this book,
I have no right to alter it in the direction of more exem-
plary beauty and deportment. He, and the fine poet, Bon-
nie Birtwistle, ask questions which were not—I'm sure—
meant to sting their old prof, only to rouse him from
office torpor. I'm grateful to them for this and for much
else.*

February 9, 1978

The day of the interview is cold, yet incongruously sunny,
a typical midwinter afternoon in Chicago. Richard Stern
arrives wearing his *bête noire* cap with as many flaps as a

---

*I suppose the key to the value system is dependence. The interviewer needs
someone else; the essayist generates all his work by himself. Physics bows to
mathematics, engineering to physics; the more apparatus, the lower the standing.
It's a leftover of a social caste system, and yet, since there's a core of fact here, the
hierarchy will persist. The core is the superiority of mind to matter.

Boeing 707 just for the sheer fun of it and because it completes the enormous impression he gives in his huge dark coat ("enormous" is one of his favorite compliments). On his coat rack, the black fur hat and the big black coat hang at attention, a spiritless *Doppelgänger*. Room 409A, Stern's large office, is on the fourth floor of Wieboldt Hall. It could be a set for *Butley*. The two big desks are cluttered with journals, books, letters, student poems, and stories. A coffin of fluorescent light supplements the gray rectangle of opaque glass in his door: across, to the south, leaded glass windows look down over a crenellated balcony into the snowy blue midway below. (It could be the setting for a Gothic novel.) To the west of his desk, a twelve-by-twenty-foot Berlin Wall of classics muffles chatter from the student coffee shop next door. But Stern does not usually look down the midway or at the shelves of hardbound masters. Instead he looks east, facing a mending wall of indispensable paperbacks and lighter reading.

A massive figure, Stern at his desk. A broad, amiable face, a sharp hawkish nose, the small eyes, dark and darting, perhaps slightly off target, will often close, expand, or stabilize during the interview. A conversation with Richard Stern has its own style of punctuation: nervous rocking in his swivel chair, pauses and explosions of laughter, a cavalcade of expressions ranging from the tyrannical to the victimized accompanied by marvelous modulations of tone, by his arms spreading in hyperbolic modesty, by his fist hammering home a point on his desk, or by his hand replacing a shock of hair, fallen in an involuntary gesture of exuberance. Then there are the two interviewers, accustomed to asking advice with the expectation of encouragement. These are familiar signs to them, familiar because

Stern's exuberance is a frequent surprise, an event by no means limited to the subject of himself.

JIM SCHIFFER

SCHIFFER: How do you feel about the various classifications of contemporary literature, the tendency to group writers as Jewish writers or Southern writers?

STERN: There's so much in the world. How are you going to get around it unless you generalize, group it and so on? The Ronald Reagan/redwood business: you've seen one redwood, you've seen them all. O.K., I've read one Jewish writer, now I don't have to read the rest of them; saves me time. We all Reader's-Digest the world. Still, it's an interesting business. After all, there's a reason why Southern writers flourish at one point, Jewish writers at another, New England writers at a third. Why today there is so much fabulous poetry written by young women.

SCHIFFER: Do you consider yourself a Jewish writer?

STERN: As for my being called a Jewish writer, along with Roth, Bellow or Malamud, I mean they are all very different, and I don't usually get included in the Hart, Schaffner & Marx (Bellow's phrase) haberdashery. Also I haven't written my "Jewish novel" yet. There are pages here and there, but I know a very different Jewish world, a very interesting world with a different hierarchy. And quite charming. I've written pages which are unpublished, and I haven't found a way of putting it all down yet. I don't know if I ever will.[†]

[†]The volume *Packages* (New York: Coward McCann and Geoghegen, 1980) contains pages of this sort, though not the ones mentioned then. Shortly after writing these pages, I gave a talk at the local Hillel chapter about the odd divi-

SCHIFFER: To my knowledge, you've never written about your childhood. Have you noticed that?

STERN: Yes.

SCHIFFER: Is there a reason for that?

STERN: Yes. My personality is not a particularly intriguing or interesting one. And, so far, it hasn't recused on me, turned on me in such a way that I have to confront it. Maybe an analyst could say I've built a Maginot line in front of it. It's a strange thing. I just don't feel intimate with myself. The first time I can get back into myself is age seven, and that was because at that point I remember saying, "I will remember this. I will remember the feel of this." And I remembered. I have certain moments which I've saved from the early years. But I don't know myself and don't much wish to. (Should I apologize to the Delphic oracle?) I'm probably not missing anything.

BIRTWISTLE: Do you write about your life now?

STERN: As far as the relationship of my life-as-a-man to my life-as-a-writer, they're hard to separate. I've written a clumsy essay on the subject. [See "Inside Narcissus."] It talks about why so many writers have such troubled lives. Why they *make trouble* in their lives and what the trouble has to do with their work. Why do writers so often hurt those they love most? And what does this have to do with their own desire to be not only good writers but more or less good people? It's a fascinating subject; I just scraped it. You'd think it would be talked about all the time, but it isn't. I do quote a wonderful passage from Conrad on it. His commitment was to vi-

---

sion in postwar American fiction between Jewish realists (Bellow, Salinger, Malamud, Roth, Algren, Mailer et al.) and non-Jewish virtuosi (Barth, Barthelme, Gass, Pynchon, Austin Wright, and Robert Coover (with whom I've worked). I mean to publish the piece in a later volume of this sort.

sual and emotional fidelity, and he talks about the pain of artistic exaggeration. An actor has to raise his voice to be heard, so he is violating naturalness. Conrad fears that such violation intoxicates. Soon the actor—the fiction writer—loves only the falsity.

SCHIFFER: How do you view the governing principle of your work? Do you base it on fidelity to personal experience and observation, do you see it as a theme or central idea, or do you approach your work in terms of story, character, and effect?

STERN: Well, let's see. I can begin with an event, a person, a "Suppose that," even a sense of form, but after the initial impulse, it's largely just writing what's fascinating me. It's mostly in rewriting that I see how things must come together. It's then that I work hardest for the symmetry and proper movement. Sometimes it means a character isn't there, sometimes there's just a deadness or a section which doesn't fit. Now I'm thinking of *Natural Shocks* as a kind of Jackson Pollock painting. The book seems a constant agitation, nothing is quite let go. Every time you think a story line will be resolved, it isn't. Something else opens up. I think it's governed by its peculiar voice, its quality of noticing and recording. Though I can also see certain types of events in it—you can call them themes—such things as the journalism-celebrity business and all the dying.

BIRTWISTLE: An English professor here at Chicago once compared *Moby Dick* to a huge cell active with different mitochondria, the many themes going on, and he remarked that the work holds together miraculously as a discrete unit centered around these various sources of energy. A similar structure, I think, shapes your book.

STERN: I think *Moby Dick* is shaped like a whale, that marvelous, intense, cerebral beginning, then that swollen middle, which for me is a mess, and then that thrashing tail of a conclusion.

BIRTWISTLE: But your book . . .

STERN: I don't know. The book may be a failure in that it doesn't hold hard to one thing. The reader says, "Give it to us, give it to us," yet I remember feeling, "No. I won't. Screw it. No. Not yet." I don't know why, but now, looking back on it a bit, I feel two things. One, that Jackson Pollockian, agitated surface somehow—luckily, perhaps—composed by certain harmonies, and two, a kind of speculative continuity which today I associate most with . . . I know this sounds ridiculously fancy . . . a solo violin or cello work by Bach, a sensuous mental pressure which keeps elaborating and building. I wish the book had more of such beautiful single-mindedness, but anyway, that's what I'm enthroning myself on today. It isn't what I was thinking about when I was doing it. And if you show up tomorrow, I might be thinking of the book as a nine-day-old fish.

SCHIFFER: I found a tension in *Natural Shocks* between the third-person narrator and Wursup. Though Wursup is a source of news, a "well-known authority," he is shown to be myopic about his own personal relationships. There are some truths in the novel, in fact, which the protagonist never learns or has to face. Were you trying to suggest by this difference between narrator and character a difference between literature and journalism, or is that far-fetched?

STERN: I don't think it is far-fetched, but I certainly can't call that an intention. I do think that the story pressure insists that Wursup is a bit stranded, more stranded than the mind which writes the book, and also a little more forlorn. Of course, how much does anyone know about himself? What self-knowledge can compare to an author's knowledge of his characters?

SCHIFFER: What about journalism's pretentions to "objective truth"?

STERN: It's the journalist's need to be comprehensive *and* interesting. Someone says of the character Mike Schilp, "He lives to convert The Everyday into The Sensational." There's the etymologic *jour*-nalistic passion to give us each day our daily news. Much life is in the margins between the *news*. Between meals, between classes, between degrees, between wives.

SCHIFFER: It seems that Wursup—the journalist—is made to descend into the domain of the novel, into the clutter of the little things in life which, of course, are also the most important things in life.

STERN: I think that is a pattern in the book. Every time Wursup is confronted with a difficult situation, he takes off to do another story. Of course, we all look for Palm Beaches, circuses, diversions; but in Wursup's case, the diversion is *life*, though at the end he has a brief vision of New York—the great altar of journalism—sinking like the lit Titanic into the dark. And he gets very quiet. I have the feeling poor Wursup has spent his soul too quickly. You can say, "O.K., at least he's educated to the point of being still," that is, he's not rushing into print about the poor girl's death, but who knows what such a fellow will do next week.

BIRTWISTLE: The most difficult part of this book for me to come to terms with is the moment when Cicia confronts Wursup with the development of her disease, what it has done to her psyche, and he leaves her.

STERN: Well, I suppose if there's a central action in the

book, it's his evasion of her. One of the little tricks of the book is to italicize a major event with a minor one. So who shows up for Cicia's death but the mother who has ignored her for years, who has always put her down, who hates her. Meanwhile, Wursup is saying, "My God, I've known this girl fewer months than this woman has had her in her body. What am *I* doing here?" Well, he knows what he is doing. I mean, this has been his invitation to the depths. He's in love not exactly with Cicia but with the pathos of her early death. He's run off from it three times, to Rome, to Bruges, and to the Maine island. But here he is taking in the strange radiance of her death. In a way, he's as bad as the mother, who scares Cicia into her last fright and then puts the sheet over her head. Wursup is not a bad fellow as people go, but this is his core. He's a flee-er. He is a burier. He's the journalistic "epitapher." Am I too hard on him now? I really like the guy.

SCHIFFER: In one of your essays, you write that Proust is your "favorite of all novelists." Could you ever see yourself attempting something enormous like *Remembrance of Things Past*?

STERN: I think a lot of writers tell themselves, "O.K., I'm a certain age, I have a certain number of years left. There is an awful lot in this world I want to write about. Do I have the guts to take the chance on one huge book?" Somehow, I have thought . . . for twenty years anyway . . . in terms of the 300–350-page manuscript, but I can conceive of at least the possibility after maybe a week of banging my head against the wall . . . of saying, "O.K., I'll take the chance, I'll go at the big one." After all, lifting yourself from the short story to the novel is a tough thing to do. I remember I wouldn't go to sleep until I had my four pages of that first novel written. But I've been thinking a little of the pleasures of an almost endless novel. My life may not be set up for it, my talent may not be up to it, but at least the thought gets me through some tough nights.

SCHIFFER: Is there anything to the claim that conditions are no longer right for a big work?

STERN: I don't believe anything of the sort. Grandeur is always a surprise. I used to think, "O.K., nobody has the confidence to be an epic writer today. Chaucer and Dante could survey their world; it was more or less comprehensible. Milton could own every book published in England in his lifetime and be an expert in eight or ten fields. Goethe had the epic confidence . . . probably misplaced. Tolstoy felt he could do the whole thing, Russia in war, Russia in peace, and then a great contemporary social novel in town, in the country, Russians at home, Russians abroad. Proust tried it by exploring his own sensibility; he probably didn't guess it was going to include so much. The people who have tried the big book in our time have not been all that successful, although they may have brilliant talents like Pynchon and Barth. The books themselves sag and get awfully simple-minded. These later writers are kind of farceurs, novelist-comedians. I'm thinking of more or less realistic writing in which the world is passed through a temperament. Of course, Anthony Powell tried it. I don't know his work very well and what I've read of it is a little soft. It does require an enormous decision. Or is it just going in and typing what you know, typing scenes, then seeing certain things growing out of them, and keeping at it, writing everything you know? I once tried an alphabet arrangement, put in all the characters I know whose names began with *A*, *B*, then C; I thought I'd work out a whole book that way. But that's the kind of thing experimental writers do. It's not for me. I didn't get very far, only far enough to dislike myself in the course of it. But I haven't entirely surrendered the big book. Come back in ten years.

SCHIFFER: In another of your essays you write that the tradition of the experimental novel has been handicapped by the achievement of Joyce. Yet it seems to me that Joyce turned to experiments because he felt the realistic novel had exhausted itself.

STERN: I think Joyce's temperament was comic and aggressive. His butt was the realistic novel. And he took on so much, answered so many questions . . . some of them raised by Flaubert. Flaubert was beginning to turn the tables on realism . . . realistically. I still think it's a matter of temperament and training. The basic question is, How does one relate to the world? Is one a Parnassian working in the salon of knowledgeable people, one's peers . . . or does one hope, perhaps absurdly and foolishly, to clarify, to put into literature, into this generalizing, comprehensive form, the novel, as much as one can about experience? And in so pleasant a way that the work is readily available to intelligent men and women who are not specialists? Yesterday I read in *Paris Review* what seemed to me an essentially foolish interview by a very intelligent man, a man whose fiction has never pleased me but whose criticism has. He said that he was now working on a particular section of a novel, trying to get the sound "Bong," a bell sound, established in it. Well, that's all very well, but what it reminded me of was the character, Herbie, in Roth's *The Professor of Desire*, whose talent is imitating defecation: premonition, rumble, process, flush. We leave him trying to perfect the wipe. Well, it's one thing to have this Jerry Lewis doing it, but to have a novelist of gift working hard at the subterranean "Bong" seems . . . well, a bit limited.

BIRTWISTLE: Do you think coteries choke literature?

STERN: Coteries are necessary fortresses for talents battered by rejection. They're important. But an audience which is a sum of coteries means Alexandria, i.e. death. A rich civilization has as many sorts of writer as possible. You don't just have a GUM, a supermarket, you have that and a bakery, and a doughnut shop, and a shop which specializes in glazed doughnuts.

There was more to the Schiffer-Birtwistle interview, but I prefer to finish off with slices from one done in the summer of 1979 (by the critics G. E. Murray and Mary Anne Tapp) and another done on the radio (by the social psychologist Milton Rosenberg and the writer-editor Elliott Anderson).

MURRAY: What attitudes, either social or intellectual, gave rise to the rumor of the demise or death, if you will, of the novel?

STERN: I would say that it's the enormous extension of nonfictional stories and the expertise with which techniques, most of them developed in the novel, have been used by sociologists, reporters, case-history writers, anthropologists like Oscar Lewis, and tape-recorder anthologists such as Studs Terkel and Max von der Gruen. I think there are other things involved. For example, the tremendous twentieth-century concern with the type of mentality which goes into construction. It's almost the displacement of construction by what Valéry in the poem "Pomegranates" calls "secret architecture," that is, not "the art that conceals art," but the story within the story. This is related to the prurient interest in personality and gossip.

At the beginning of the century, we had the great museums and scholarly assemblages. Then we had the technology of collection which enabled individuals to collect the great works of the world in the form of reproductions, records, inexpensive editions. These imaginary, or rather real, personal museums generate in sensitive people the desire to know what these things have in common, what lies behind them, what kind of mentality is there. Can the traditional novel satisfy this kind of mentality? Sometimes not. So we have the development of the "Joycettes," those who, in various ways, try to express the ways human beings have had their experience *written about*. . . . The concern with language and techniques of fiction is related to the belief that realities are as much created by the words and conventions which represent them, as by anything else *out there*. In physics, we had and have the great debate between the Planck-Einstein people and those who follow Mach, Bohr, and Heisenberg. . . .

MURRAY: Let me shift gears on you for a while. John Gardner, in *Moral Fiction*, suggests that lack of first-rate literature may lead to a sick society.

STERN: I think that the finest art, and the finest moments in oneself, come from a layer which overrides any judicial, moral, or other humane structure. It may come from the wildest part of nature, and if it has social application, it is of a complexity beyond what John Gardner describes in *Moral Fiction*. It becomes a visible and beautiful and releasing expression of a time. It takes its place in the richest human tradition, the mental tradition, which is connected with language, and the history of this richest of art forms—prose fiction. Its social application has to do with the refreshment of language—so that language does not become a dike against original expression—and behavior—so that behavior doesn't become calcified. Thus, in a sense, it's social lubricant. Above all, the creations allow other human beings the sense of new personality, the artist in the art beyond "his own personality."

This is the highest sort of morality. That is why a wicked man can be a moral writer. Had *Mein Kampf* been written by a man of literary genius, despite its frightful opinons—it could conceivably be as "morally" valuable as *The Divine Comedy*.

MURRAY: Is there such a thing as an academic novelist?

STERN: I think so, yes, but it can be said that the *Odyssey*, written by a close student of the *Iliad*, is the first academic novel.

STERN: I suppose it's consoling to believe in the survival of personality. Or if you feel that you'll be joined with a dead loved one somewhere, sometime. I think many people know that the way they die is going to be significant. Even for themselves, death is a kind of staging of what they have in them. Perhaps a certain theatrical power can make death very remarkable for the dying. Perhaps a person pares down those things which have been excrescences and decides his death will be the perfect sculpture, the perfect declaration, of his being. But in the novel [*Natural Shocks*], the last words of the most significant die-er are, "You're scaring me." Death is one of the recurrent human subjects. I say recurrent, because interest in it as a subject is sporadic. It comes in periods. At one time, there are graveyard poets, another time great graveyard preachers. John Donne trains himself for death by trying out his coffin; he tried to inoculate himself against death. In the Enlightenment, you have the rational, that is, stoic deaths of the Houyhnhnms in fiction and David Hume in reality. The protagonist of this novel has discovered certain death fashions, and his conclusion is bleak. Death is not the Reaper for him. The only thing he can come up with is Death the Sniper. I suppose some people can float to their death or drink themselves out of consciousness, and now, perhaps, many can narcoticize themselves into extinction. But at least the living can say, "To philosophize is to learn to die." And that, I suppose, is a bit of what we're doing now.

ROSENBERG: I think of the Hemingway sort of vision which is that life is never more vividly and fully experienced than when one seeks, by will, the danger of death, if only then to master that danger.

STERN: It's the existential notion. Nietzsche said the "weightiest human experience"—he called it—involved living as if your every action were eternally recurrent. So you'd have to go through what you'd just gone through again and again. Your choice was permanent. In a sense, that trivializes mortality. It's another narcotic, something that shows up in this little novel, the relationship of personality celebrated by practically everything around us —in particular, all the story media—to extinction.

The urge to exist as a complete personality, to make a passionate impression on the world, has a powerful relationship to the total extinction of personality. No recurrence or resurrection. So the way one dies is an intimate part of the expression of oneself. Wursup talks of the most vivid personalities—Dr. Johnson, Goethe, Freud—

and says they were the people most terrified by death. They had the worst cases of *Todangst.*

Q[†]: What is the purpose of the novel? What does the novelist have in mind? Is he trying to express a view of life or is he writing for an audience or is he writing for himself?

STERN: Well, a number of things. I do think the idea is to make something very beautiful that's never before existed on earth, something that's very special and moving to people. It's moving through the use of this medium— story language—which is usually treated with great intensity, so that the language itself has a kind of power which has never existed before. Nobody's quite spoken, written, sounded like this. So there's a new sound in the world, just as if somebody invented a new type of orange. And for the individual who's doing this kind of work, it's a medium in which most of himself can get most interestingly—I don't know about expressed—but created. He creates a more interesting version of himself, perhaps a bearable version of himself. I should think those are some of the purposes of the so-called serious novel. Maybe the word *serious* is wrong. One of the things these novels do is bounce around and be amusing. The story energy frequently touches off the comic side of the most desperate events.

[†]A question called in by radio audience member.